Beckett Beyond the Normal

For Aaron Kushner

Beckett Beyond the Normal

Edited by Seán Kennedy

EDINBURGH
University Press

Edinburgh University Press is one of the leading university presses in the UK. We publish academic books and journals in our selected subject areas across the humanities and social sciences, combining cutting-edge scholarship with high editorial and production values to produce academic works of lasting importance. For more information visit our website: edinburghuniversitypress.com

© editorial matter and organisation Seán Kennedy, 2020, 2022
© the chapters their several authors, 2020, 2022

Edinburgh University Press Ltd
The Tun – Holyrood Road,
12(2f) Jackson's Entry,
Edinburgh EH8 8PJ

First published in hardback by Edinburgh University Press 2020

Typeset in 10.5/13 pt Sabon by
Servis Filmsetting Ltd, Stockport, Cheshire

A CIP record for this book is available from the British Library

ISBN 978 1 4744 6046 0 (hardback)
ISBN 978 1 4744 6047 7 (paperback)
ISBN 978 1 4744 6048 4 (webready PDF)
ISBN 978 1 4744 6049 1 (epub)

The right of Seán Kennedy to be identified as the editor of this work has been asserted in accordance with the Copyright, Designs and Patents Act 1988, and the Copyright and Related Rights Regulations 2003 (SI No. 2498).

Contents

Abbreviations		vii
	'Here all is strange': Beckett beyond the normal Seán Kennedy	1
1	Murphy and the Tao of Autism Joseph Valente	16
2	Narrating Disruption: Realist Fiction and the Politics of Form in *Watt* William Davies	33
3	'no human shape': Unformed Life in *The Unnamable* Byron Heffer	47
4	Beckett, Evangelicalism and the Biopolitics of Famine Seán Kennedy	62
5	'He wants to know if it hurts!': Suffering beyond Redemption in *Waiting for Godot* Hannah Simpson	79
6	'as if the sex matters': Beckett, Barthes and *Endgame* in Love James Brophy	90
7	Beckett's Queer Time of *Défaillance*: Ritual and Resistance in *Happy Days* Nic Barilar	105
8	Beckett's Safe Words: Normalising Torture in *How It Is* Dominic Walker	117

Bibliography 133
Notes on Contributors 149
Index 151

Abbreviations

D   Samuel Beckett, *Dream of Fair to Middling Women* (1992)
E1   Samuel Beckett, 'Endgame', in *The Complete Dramatic Works* (2006)
E2   Samuel Beckett, *Endgame*, ed. R. MacDonald (2009)
HD   Samuel Beckett, *Happy Days* (2013)
HII   Samuel Beckett, *How It Is: A Critical-Genetic Edition*, ed. E. O'Reilly (2001)
LD   Roland Barthes, *A Lover's Discourse: Fragments* (1978)
LI   Samuel Beckett, *The Letters of Samuel Beckett: Vol. I, 1929–1940* (2009)
LII   Samuel Beckett, *The Letters of Samuel Beckett: Vol. II, 1941–1956* (2011)
LIII   Samuel Beckett, *The Letters of Samuel Beckett: Vol. III, 1957–1965* (2014)
LIV   Samuel Beckett, *The Letters of Samuel Beckett: Volume IV, 1966–1989* (2016)
M   Samuel Beckett, *Murphy* (1938)
P   'Pim', Notebook 6, Samuel Beckett Collection, Harry Ransom Center, University of Texas at Austin
Q   Ato Quayson, 'Autism, narrative and emotion: on Samuel Beckett's *Murphy*' (2010)
U   Samuel Beckett, *The Unnamable* (2010)
W   Samuel Beckett, *Watt* (2009)
WG   Samuel Beckett, 'Waiting for Godot', in *The Complete Dramatic Works* (2006)
WMS   The *Watt* Manuscripts, Samuel Beckett Collection, Harry Ransom Center, University of Texas at Austin

'Here all is strange':
Beckett beyond the Normal

Seán Kennedy

[A] normal literature while welcoming the criticism of outsiders neither lives nor dies by such criticism. It abides the judgement of its own people, and by that judgement lives or dies. If this literature then be not a normal literature it is not a national literature, for normal and national are synonymous in literary criticism.

(Corkery 1931: 15)

In a remarkable letter of 1935, Beckett described to Thomas McGreevy the crippling propensity for personal morbidity that sent him to London for psychoanalysis:

For years I was unhappy, consciously and deliberately ever since I left school and went into T.C.D., so that I isolated myself more and more, undertook less and less and lent myself to a crescendo of disparagement of others and myself. But in all that there was nothing that struck me as morbid. The misery and the solitude and apathy and the sneers were the elements of an index of superiority and guaranteed the feeling of arrogant 'otherness', which seemed right and natural and as little morbid as the ways in which it was not so much expressed as implied and reserved and kept available for a possible utterance in the future. It was not until that way of living, or rather negation of living, developed such terrifying physical symptoms that it could no longer be pursued that I became aware of anything morbid in myself. (LI 258-9)

Earlier, in preparation for *Dream of Fair to Middling Women* (1932), Beckett had studied Max Nordau's *Degeneration*, in which a generalised definition of degeneracy, as 'morbid deviation from an original type' ([1892] 1993: 16), framed a six-hundred-page account of the causes, condition and characteristics of the degenerate artist. Drawing together various threads from criminology, medicine and literature, degeneration theory provided an alarming account of the decline of Western civilisation. Rooted in Lamarckianism, it proposed that dysfunctional traits were not only heritable but increased in debilitating power over time (Valente 2013: 383). Society was dying, and progress – city life, stress, narcotics – was killing it. It was a sustaining paradox of the discourse that degeneration was being ceaselessly generated, but it was precisely the ambient nature of the threat, 'both hereditary and contagious' (Valente 2013: 383), that provided the basis for conservative scaremongering. Beckett found the book exasperating, as anyone who has read it will understand, but he also recognised aspects of himself in its pages, noting down traits and tendencies, such as 'aboulia' (lack of will), that reflected his own symptoms (Nordau [1892] 1993: 20; Pilling 1999: 89).

These symptoms, he learned later, were compromise formations – coded betrayals – necessarily conflicted expressions of unconsciously conflicted loyalties (Freud [1905] 1979: 79; Phillips). He was besieged by his own body, by 'sweats & shudders & panics & rages & rigors & heart-burstings' (LI 258), and turned to art to save his sanity. Creative writing offered a space to explore and displace his anxieties, recasting personal struggles in barely fictionalised episodes of comic farce. He refused McGreevy's offer of instructive materials – Thomas à Kempis and the like – on the basis that they would make no difference. Or, as he put it, no 'philosophical or ethical or Christlike' instruction could 'redeem a composition that was invalid from the word "go" and has to be broken up altogether' (LI 259). If we think about Beckett beyond the normal, then, we are simply considering him where he was, or felt himself to be, from the beginning of his (artistic) life: beyond the normal and, until he entered psychoanalysis, beyond redemption too.

A number of essays in this volume challenge what we might call the 'redemptive perversion' in Beckett studies. As Hannah Simpson notes here, Beckett coined the phrase to describe misguided productions of his plays in England, but there has been an equivalent tendency among critics. We have tended to recuperate his work to ethical purpose. Leo Bersani (1990) queries the ethical value that accrues to art in this way, and, in Beckett's case, the more one thinks about it, the odder it seems (Critchley 2014: 211). There is an unremitting bleakness to the *oeuvre* that makes it a strange place to seek consolation. Reading *Malone Dies*, James McNaughton has demonstrated Beckett's scepticism with regard to art's redemptive potential (2018: 79–105), while anyone who has read *Murphy* (Beckett 1938; hereafter M) will know how he felt about life in Max Weber's iron cage: 'Here, for what might have been six months he had eaten, drunk, slept, and put his clothes on and off, in a medium-sized cage of northwestern aspect' (M 5). Overall the sense is that Beckett was exercised by modernity's normalising regimes but wary of claims that art could get us beyond them. For this reason, Byron Heffer (2019) has queried the justness of our attempts to link him to emancipatory resistance. Rather, says Nic Barilar here, in a reading of *Happy Days*, Beckett enacts the *limits* of such resistance. In *The Queer Art of Failure* (2011), Jack Halberstam sought to redeem queer failure as success in the guise of resistance to normalising routines. Failure, he suggested, is something queers do exceptionally well (2011: 3). Barilar refuses any such recuperation. Far from being an *homage* to queer failure, *Happy Days* is an enactment of the regulative regimes of the normal. In *Happy Days*, the routines that Winnie makes her own merely serve to compound her servitude to the mores of commodity culture. In this view, we are all stuck: Winnie in her mound, the audience in their seats, and all of us in a society of instrumentalised relations. Beckett enacts our entrapment by, not liberation from, deadening routine. Whatever his art offers us in the circumstances, it is precisely not redemption.

In 2004, Peter Boxall noted an 'extraordinary instance of mass denial' of the homoerotic in Beckett studies (2004: 110). It was a stunning insight. Here, James Brophy notes its restrictive basis. The work is not homoerotic merely, but queer: what Freud would call perverse. Reading Clov's great final soliloquy, Brophy goes beyond queer theory, and homoerotic readings of *Endgame* specifically, to read it as a play about love. Roland Barthes's *A Lover's Discourse* (1978) reconceives love as a solitary, socially deprived state. Brophy provides an exquisitely bleak portrayal of love as a condition of extreme solitude. What is finally 'radical about the queerness that pervades' Beckett's world, he suggests, is that 'the heterosexual/homosexual binary is reduced to essentially nothing'. Queerness is not relational (or anti-relational) but a condition that is 'experiential and *individual*'. It is 'beyond any remaining networks of normality'. Love is a queer investment that 'produces nothing beyond itself'.

For Hannah Simpson, any search for redemption in Beckett's work merely distorts his pitiless portrayals of human suffering. Predisposed to a Schopenhauerian view, Beckett's experiences during World War II confirmed a suspicion that, as human beings, we suffer alone. Citing Elaine Scarry's work on pain's unsharability, Simpson reads *Waiting for Godot* as a dramatisation of suffering, not an account of how it might bring us together. Beckett is mimicking the compassion fatigue that he witnessed in wartime France, not offering up pain as a means to reconciliation. His characters suffer, and cause each other to suffer, in ways that are beyond redemption. To ignore this is to betray his vision of human cruelty.

Torture is, perhaps, the limit case of human cruelty, and, artistically, Beckett was fascinated by it. It shows up regularly in his work, where we have tended to think of it as a metaphor for something else, most often aesthetics (Miller 2000: 255). In 2017, Emilie Morin brought the issue back into focus with a dazzling account of Beckett's response to the Algerian War (2017: 184–237). For Morin, Beckett's writings of the 1950s and 1960s are in a sustained dialogue with events in Algeria (220). Dominic Walker joins the debate here, in response to David Lloyd's (2010) Kantian reading of *How It Is* (1961). Lloyd reads the book in formalist terms, and finds no evidence that Beckett is referring to French torturers in particular (2010: 211). Walker contests that reading, noting specific references to Algeria but also, and more uncomfortably, to Beckett's private life. Both are condensed in the acronym PAM. For Walker, *How It Is* offers a 'provocative normalisation of torture' that leaves us with a number of awkward questions about the aesthetics of violation.

So much for the culture of redemption. In becoming a writer, we must concede, Beckett did not hope to redeem the world. But, we might add, he *did* hope to redeem himself: from his morbidity, from its symptoms, from the 'pain and monstrosity and incapacitation' it caused him (LI 258). When he rejected McGreevy's kind offer of spiritual assistance, he gave, by way of explanation, a pathological variant on Joyce's *non serviam*: 'When I cannot answer for myself, and do not dispose of myself, how can I serve?' (LI 258). Things were out of control. He was not the master of his own house. The problem was not moral, but psychological: 'Will the demon – pretiosa margarita! – disable me any less with sweats & shudders & panics [...] if my motives are disinterested?' (LI 258). In effect, Beckett turned to one kind of composition (literary) in the hope of redeeming another (his own) and the results were beyond the normal from the outset. Invalid from the word go. Condensed in that word were medical, moral, even aesthetic implications. And all of them were in the mix at the time. Not much of what Beckett wrote in this period made sense seen from any perspective other than his own (or even his own).

But when his brother, Frank, asked in exasperation, 'Why can't you write the way people want?', his answer was simple: integrity. In the sense of structural integrity: of a shape that cannot be changed. 'I replied that I could only write the one way, i.e. the best I could' (LI 366). If the results disgusted his family, what disgusted him was artifice. He was sick, he reasoned, his writings should be too. That is what artistic integrity meant. Hence the obscure reference to his poems doing 'the work of the abscess' (LI 134). They were an aspect of his struggle with disease. Instead of the 'negation of living' that was his symptoms (LI 258), Beckett pursued a negation of his symptoms in writing. This did not redeem them, necessarily, but it did offer him a sense of purpose. Where art was concerned, as opposed to religion, even as he could not control himself, he *could* put himself in service to something: artistic truth.

Beckett's encounter with psychoanalysis offered a model for these preoccupations. In *Three Essays on the Theory of Sexuality*, Freud uses the language of 'instinct' and 'drive', of 'discharge' and 'excitation', to characterise human sexuality ([1905] 1979: 83). And Beckett wanted his writings to have the integrity of an instinct. He talked insistently in this period of his works as emissions or discharges. As 'vomit, shit, slobber and tears' (Salisbury and Code 2016: 222). He thought of his compositions, the best of them anyway, as by-products: 'involuntary exonerations' (LI 88). Writing was 'a process of excitation occurring in an organ' (Freud [1905] 1979: 83). It should 'strive to obtain an expression [. . .] appropriate to [its] emotional discharge' (Freud [1905] 1979: 78). Hence, 'The Beckett bowel books' (LI 383). Anything else was 'fraudulent' (LI 134). It might read respectably, or please his publisher, but it would not be *his*. The analogy was not perfect: one cannot draft an ejaculation, for example, or rehearse a turd. But it got him going. It got him beyond paralysis.

Psychosexually, then, the model was Freud. Ethically, the model was Joyce. When asked how Joyce had positioned himself politically – what he was 'against' and what 'for' – Beckett replied, 'Beyond it all' (LIV 67). And that meant being beyond enlistment, beyond conventional morality. The artist did not write in opposition to such things, but beyond them. However, this entailed neither amorality nor nihilism. Joyce's influence on him, he remarked in 1954, was precisely 'moral': 'He gave me, without in the least wishing to do so, an insight into what the words "to be an artist" mean' (LII 463–4). In the 1930s, the writings that pleased Beckett were not always pleasant, or coherent, or agreeable to others, but they 'recommended themselves' to him 'in as much as "true"' (LI 87).

An obvious problem with this approach, its disingenuous aspect perhaps, was the issue of form. Can artistic form ever be *im*mediate? Nordau felt so. His degeneration theory was an aesthetics of form, physical as well as literary, in which art's classical forms were mere epiphenomena of rational thought (Kennedy and Valente, np). For Nordau, thought always takes the correct form, provided one is thinking correctly. Beckett, for his part, had little interest in classical form. But neither, as Salisbury and Code observe, was he interested in automatic writing (2016: 211). Rather, he eschewed 'intentional capacity' while retaining the sense of an 'affective life' hoping for expression (219). So, while there were all sorts of things about degeneration theory that Beckett rejected, where he could not extract a principle of moral integrity from Thomas à Kempis (LI 257), he did wrangle a theory of artistic integrity from Joyce and Freud and Nordau (Kennedy and Valente, n.p.). Nordau had suggested degenerate artists were helpless before the outpourings of their diseased constitutions, and, for a time, that was how Beckett chose to see things also: 'Exeo in a spasm' (Beckett 2012: 6). In *Dream of Fair to Middling Women* (unpublished 1932), and *More Pricks than Kicks* (1934), he frames his alter-ego, Belacqua Shuah, as a post-war degenerate (Purcell 2015). Since the Romantics, at least, it was suggested that art should emerge organically as from nature. Beckett made a similar case for the degenerate constitution. He accepted the picture of himself as 'morbid' and made to express himself as freely, and fitfully, as possible. 'The mouth must stutter or rest', he told McGreevy, 'and it takes a more stoical mouth than mine to rest' (LI 134). Whether or not any of this was true mattered less than what it made possible artistically. The goal was 'spontaneous combustion of the spirit' (LI 134).

For Freud, 'symptoms involve suffering'; they dominate the patient's social life ([1905] 1979: 80). By his own admission, Beckett's 'disable[d]' him (LI 258). And perhaps the most difficult thing he learned from psychoanalysis was that symptoms are where desire and disability converge. That, at any rate, was Freud's theory:

> all my experience shows that these psychoneuroses are based on instinctual sexual forces. By this I do not merely mean that the energy of the sexual instinct makes a contribution to the forces that maintain the pathological manifestations (the symptoms). I mean expressly to assert that that contribution is the most important and only constant source of energy of the neurosis and that in consequence the sexual life of the persons in question is expressed – whether exclusively or principally or only partly – in these symptoms. As I have put it elsewhere, the symptoms constitute the sexual activity of the patient. (Freud [1905] 1979: 77)

In this reading, the source of Beckett's disability was his desire: his symptoms *were* his sex life. He was ill, certainly, but his symptoms, and his inability to get beyond them, betrayed an unwillingness to relinquish them. Above all, what he was suffering from was the wish to fall ill, a wish that was more acceptable than the one it had displaced: his ambivalent love-hate for mother (Kennedy 2019a). In psychoanalytic perspective, Beckett discovered, he was both disabled and perverted by incestuous desire.

By this time, not the least thing that interested him about psychoanalysis was its account of the perversions. Before Freud, degeneration theory had dominated sexology. The sexual instinct *was* the genital instinct. Perversions were simply 'morbid modifications' of it (in Davidson 2001: 75). Genital sex – being regenerative – was natural, and any deviation from that an aberration in nature. As Albert Moll insisted in 1891, 'we ought to consider the absence of heterosexual desires morbid' (in Davidson 2001: 76). This, we note, is a moral injunction. It captures the dual mandate, ethical as well as physiological, of degeneration theory. In the *Three Essays*, however, Freud rejects the degeneration hypothesis. He collapses the distinction between perversion and normalcy, seeing the one as inherent to the other ([1905] 1979: 74). By dividing the sexual instinct in terms of aim and object, he dismantles genital instinct as the sole vector of libido. Anything can become a sexual object, and libido aims everywhere (46). Perverse desire 'alongside' genital desire is nothing to worry about, Freud suggests (74). Sex is practically unthinkable without it. Normally, a host of factors, many of them socially cultivated, work to delimit perversity (74). To differing degrees, therefore, we are all perverse in our relationship to 'the normal sexual aim' (74). There is no original type. Or rather, what *is* original is perversion.

This is a supposition that, quite obviously, implicated heterosexuality too. For Freud, heterosexuality is as morbidly preoccupied, as in need of explanation, as anything else. In *Three Essays*, however, he both undermines the clinical basis for perversion and continues to use the concept anyway (Davidson 2001: 63). Not for the first time, he hesitates to accept his own conclusions: to go beyond the normal. Freud's findings gestured irresistibly beyond genital sexuality, but he couldn't quite go there. This is one place where he ran up against the limits of his own preconceptions: what Arnold Davidson calls the 'automatisms' of his *mentalité* (2001: 62). Almost despite himself, Freud identifies certain practices – coprophagy and necrophilia, specifically – as 'truly' perverse acts in which all obstacles to perversion – 'shame, disgust, horror or pain' – are overcome ([1905] 1979: 74). In Tim Dean's brilliant reading, such perverts are, in a strict sense, Freud's ultimate lovers, since they go to 'astonishing lengths' to override the forces that (ought to) dissuade them (Freud

([1905] 1979: 74). By the strict logic of the drives, shit-eating is not a perversion but the 'triumph of love' (Dean 2000: 264–8). For Freud, this was not easily accepted.

Beckett, by contrast, moved more quickly into the queer spaces left by *Three Essays*. In part one of that work, 'The sexual aberrations', Freud had clarified 'the proverbial durability of first loves' in notable terms: '*on revient toujours à ses premiers amours*' (Freud [1905] 1979: 67). Beckett agreed, and in his story of that name, written in 1946 but suppressed until 1969, the narrator – already given to pissing on gravestones – is prompted to eat shit as proof of his love for Lulu (1995: 34). David Lloyd reads this, in classical Freudian terms, as evidence of a 'negative dialectic of identity' (1995: 49). But it also exemplifies the erotic possibilities unleashed in *Three Essays* before Freud retreated to the normal logic of perversion. A determinedly psychoanalytic text, *Premier Amour* combines exile from mothers and motherlands with coprophilia and desecration of graves in a blend of outrage that might shock anybody. The Irish as a nation of shit-sniffers. Hence, perhaps, its suppression until the Nobel Prize: a rare example of self-censorship (Knowlson 1996: 574).

In 1994, W. J. McCormack offered a political reading of Beckett's symptoms as evidence of his alienation from the Irish Free State (1994: 390). He surmised that an amount of Beckett's psychological unsettlement might be indexed to his status as colonial settler. Unable to integrate into the new Ireland, Beckett was also unwilling to behave how 'his own people' wanted, and it all got under his skin. Certainly, if Beckett's symptoms were one place that sex and disability converged in the 1930s, Irish politics was another. Mitchell and Snyder (2015) call it ablenationalism. In discourses of national regeneration, human validity is indexed directly to sexual fertility and/or a capacity for productive labour: to production and reproduction. Disability, like perversion, is abjected in the process of national self-definition (Purcell 2019). Both sex and disability tear at the veil of normalcy that cloaks compulsory ablebodiedness and compulsory heterosexuality as founding myths of the nation state. Unfit bodies and unfit desires, often seen to converge in disability anyway (Mollow 2012: 286), are pathologised in pursuit of fitting emblems. The normate gets to be representative (Garland-Thompson 1997: 6). 'The disabled' does not. At stake is what form the nation (but also its art, its bodies) might take.

Published in 1931, Daniel Corkery's *Synge and Anglo-Irish Literature* was one of the first works to address what Irish art should look like after independence. Positing an exact coincidence between normalcy and nationality, Corkery highlights the distorting impact of colonialism on Irish letters. Marred by 'alien' themes and preoccupations, literature under the Union was that of an occupying class, or produced for alien markets, or symptomatic of internalised oppression: 'an alien medium' for native self-apprehension (1931: 15). Independence meant speaking with insight to the three great themes of Irish life: 'religion, nationalism and the land' (22). Corkery highlights the role played by literature in the normalisation of occupation. But also the 'integrative' function of aesthetics in decolonisation: as an institution meant to develop ethical identity (Lloyd 1995: 42–7). To institute norms of form. Beckett understood the darker implications of this, as Lloyd (Maedhbh) Houston has shown. When asked to write about Ireland's censorship legislation in 1935, his first instinct was to consult the new Criminal Law Amendment Bill (Houston 2019: 28).

James Smith's (2004) pioneering work on this bill confirms, in an Irish context, Foucault's analysis of a 'normalising society' where any identification of social norms produces, of necessity, a 'residue' of inassimilable elements that must be purged (2008: 53–4): 'fallen women', queers, republicans, vagrants, asylum seekers – all to be 'taken care of' so that the nation might thrive. In Ireland, care took many forms, but confinement was the preferred option, leading to the vast 'architecture of containment' that has existed ever since (Smith 2004; Lentin 2016). At various times, this has included both the official institutions of the State (prisons and reform schools) and the unofficial sites run by Irish churches (Magdalen laundries, mother and baby homes, orphanages) – as well as the various medical institutions (psychiatric hospitals, county homes, lunatic asylums) that took on the task of managing abnormality. To these, we must add the various internment and concentration camps that have housed military and paramilitary prisoners north and south of the border. Many of these institutions pre-existed the Irish state but were easily repurposed to the task of defending Irish society. Confinement could function outside the law and was justified, as Foucault suggests, by the need to 'correct, to improve, to lead to repentance' all those deemed a threat to the nation (1997: 53). Ireland needed to regenerate. What it did not need was to be weighed down by 'abject populations peripheral to the project of living' (Snyder and Mitchell 2010: 119). When the Carrigan Report (1931) suggested an alarming rise in assaults on vulnerable populations in Ireland after independence the data was suppressed on the basis that it would 'rejoice our enemies' (Smith 2004: 217).

So much for home. Yet whenever he left Ireland, whether to visit Germany in 1936–7 (Nixon 2011), or to live and work in Paris (Gibson 2015), Beckett found some version of these same themes playing out: national health, national art, national re/degeneration. In Nazi Germany, too, art was condemned to play the role of integrative propaganda: to express and embody national ideals (Michaud 2004). In Vichy France, some of the most baleful aspects of life in Ireland, including ablenationalism, were matters of public discourse (Gibson 2010b, 2015). Wherever Beckett went, it seemed, the emphasis was on the fit and the unfit: on fitness and fitting in. He was living through the great paroxysm of purity that brought the biopolitical project of the modern nation state to its culmination in the death camps of Hitler and Stalin, and, against this backdrop, his own relationship to art changed. It was the cataclysmic move to sacrifice 'degenerates' – the disabled, the Roma, Jews, homosexuals, alcoholics, prostitutes – at the altar of progress that gave the twentieth century its enduring shape, and it changed Beckett's outlook forever. For one thing, artistic integrity was no longer enough. It was no longer sufficient to be simply true to one's self.

For Byron Heffer here, *The Unnamable* is what happens to Beckett after Hitler. Nazism is a racism of form – of aesthetic impropriety – with deep roots in Plato. Not all are born human. 'One has to be part of true humanity' (Forti 2006: 23). Race 'brings order to the chaotic world of appearances' (18). Good form implies the fertility, health and moral integrity of an individual, their soul and its race. It is lookism with a vengeance. The body is the mirror of the soul, the soul is race seen from the inside (14), while deformity betrays what the degenerate is and ought to be. It was a Nazi 'pseudometaphysics' (16), but no less powerful for that. The goal was 'perfect identity of body and soul' (18). In Heffer's account, Beckett's unnamable is a degenerate artist playing at biopolitics: making things live and letting them die. His amorphous narrator models varieties of unformed life to explore the 'homicidal will-to-form' of fascist aesthetics.

William Davies, extending work by James McNaughton (2018: 60–79), confirms that Beckett wrote his Irish Big House novel, *Watt*, with an eye to Germany. Having narrowly escaped arrest in Paris, Beckett was chary of progress narratives. *Watt* engages Daniel Corkery's idea of the telos of the novel as the telos of the nation, but only to disrupt that homology. And it does so at the level of form as well as content. It is not just that the Lynch family cannot get it together to realise their millennial hopes for Ireland, their hopes are themselves linked to a critique of Nazism at the level of narrative form. Disruption underpins what passes for progress in Beckett's *sui generis* masterpiece. He is mimicking the narrative strategies of Nazism. But he is also modelling aspects of complicity (McNaughton 2018: 156). Developing this claim, my own essay examines Beckett's response to genocide against British relief policies during the Irish famine. Where McNaughton reads *Endgame* in light of the food politics of Hitler and Stalin (2018: 137–65), I examine their impact on Beckett's self-assessment as a colonial settler. The grandson of a grain merchant to boot (Knowlson 1996: 2).

In all of this, the work of W. B. Yeats is a crucial mediator: the place where fascist sympathies, Big House biopolitics, and blood and soil republicanism converge in ablenationalist fantasy. As far as 'pseudometaphysics' go, there are few works to match *A Vision* (1937). Combining mysticism with mathematics at dazzling altitude, it is Yeats's final abdication of his great theme of responsibility. As it turns out, we are not finally responsible for our condition, which depends on what phase of history we are living through. Like the Nazis in Heffer's account, Yeats envisaged history as a will-to-form. Matter is constantly being shaped and reshaped, and much of what passes for life is little more than ordure. By 1935–6, Yeats was decrepit himself, and so *A Vision* displaces responsibility for degeneration onto the stars. Ascendancy as astrology. We may live heroically – 'antithetically' – but that in itself does not deliver us from 'the Body of Fate'. Nietzsche is a case in point:

> Nietzsche is born,
> because the hero's crescent is the twelfth.
> And yet, twice born, twice buried, grow he must,
> Before the full moon, helpless as a worm. (Yeats [1937] 1962: 60)

'Degenerate form is always an undoing of form', as Heffer puts it. Worm, who reappears in *The Unnamable*, is Yeats's image for biological matter that has barely attained, or retained, the status of life. As race and individual, we circle between formlessness and embodied perfection. In Phase 1, the body is 'undifferentiated, dough-like' (Yeats [1937] 1962: 183). In phase 15, 'every bodily form is loved' (136). By phase 26, deformity is quasi-inevitable: 'The Hunchback is his own Body of Fate' (178). By the end, we are back at the beginning: 'Deformed beyond deformity, unformed/insipid as the dough before it is baked' (63). In 1934, Beckett had mocked *A Vision* in 'Echo's Bones' (Kennedy 2014b: 240). He needed to move beyond mockery now.

Darren Gribben has identified 1946, and the short radio piece 'The Capital of the Ruins', as evidence of an epiphany on Beckett's part. It was while working to reconstruct Saint-Lô, a town 'bombed out of existence in one night', that he discovered 'a time-honoured conception of humanity in ruins' (Beckett 1995: 277–8). The devastation was total but, in Gribben's reading, also a source of uplift: Beckett 'testifies to a perseverance that undermines the destruction' (Gribben 2008: 265). If this seems difficult to envisage – perseverance undermining destruction – doubtful claims are made on the strength of it: 'in *Happy Days*, Winnie's fortitude almost appears to conquer her confinement' (Gribben 2008: 265). A significant qualification, given that she is being buried alive. But it shows how tenacious the redemptive perversion can be. It is as if we are predisposed to ignore the bleakness that Beckett puts before us. That we find it 'unacceptable' (Heffer 2019: 79). Nevertheless, Gribben is right to suggest something profound happens around 1946. Beckett has 'an inkling of the terms in which our condition is to be thought again' (1995: 278). And it has something to do with disability.

As with torture, disability in Beckett studies is often taken as a metaphor for something else, the post-war human condition, for example (Davidson 2007: 15). In Saint-Lô, the issue is more concrete:

> I think I am right in saying that the number of inpatients (mixed) is in the neighbourhood of 90. As for others, it is a regular thing, according to recent reports, for as many as 200 to be seen in the out-patients department in a day. Among such ambulant cases a large number are suffering from scabies and other diseases of the skin, the result no-doubt of malnutrition or an ill-advised diet. Accident cases are frequent. Masonry falls when least expected, children play with detonators and demining continues. (Beckett 1995: 276)

No metaphors here. In Beckett's work after 1946, disability is ubiquitous, but it has taken a long time for that to come into view. Important work has been done (Bixby 2018; Davidson 2007; Levin 2018; Purcell 2015, 2019; Quayson 2010), particularly in the medical humanities (Barry et al. 2016; Maude 2008; Salisbury 2008), but we need to think more about how and why Beckett goes beyond the normate, that is, beyond ablebodiedness. It is not just that disability features more prominently in the works after the war. They are spaces of near-universal disability. 'Disability ensembles' (Snyder and Mitchell 2006: 175). If *Happy Days*, for example, captures 'the signifying affect of disabled bodies' (Snyder and Mitchell

2006: 164), it also diminishes the corporeal boundaries that delimit them as such. 'Here all is strange', as Winnie observes (2010a: 25). In this way, Beckett translates disabled bodies from 'pathologized objects in a normate world to a mode of worlding unto themselves' (Kennedy and Valente, n.p.). As in Freud's *Three Essays*, there is no normal, and 'when disability is the norm', says Michael Davidson, 'the human condition must be revised in terms of non-traditional bodies and sensoria' (2007: 15).

For Davidson, who underlines the significance of disability only to recast it, once again, as figurative, Beckett's disabled partnerships offer a parable about the limits of agency and community in the post-ableist era. In critique of social contract theory, Beckett portrays the human condition as one of mutual, more or less abject, co-dependency (15). More radically, in his second seminar, Jacques Lacan uses 'the blind-man and the paralytic' to characterise human subjectivity itself:

> Subjectivity on the level of the ego is comparable to this couple [. . .]. The subjective half of the pre-mirror experience is the paralytic, who cannot move about by himself except in an uncoordinated and clumsy way. What masters him is the image of the ego, which is blind, and which carries him [. . .]. And the paralytic, whose perspective this is, can only identify with his unity in a fascinated fashion, in the fundamental immobility whereby he finishes up corresponding to the gaze he is under, the blind gaze. (1988: 50)

Such is the basis of Lacan's antihumanism. Accession to subjectivity *itself* disables the human subject. This has all sorts of exciting implications for Beckett's work, but we must also remark its reliance on ableist metaphors. As Shelley Tremain (2017) points out, Western philosophy (and we can add psychoanalysis) has relied, since its inception, on disability to shore up its account of normal functioning. For Tremain, 'the disabled' know all about life beyond the normal, because they are brought into being in its very delimitation. In the work of Leo Bersani and Lee Edelman, for example, disability recurs 'to figure the self-rupturing aspects of sex' (Mollow 2012: 301). Sex *is* disability. Or rather, both terms are used, often interchangeably, to describe the same 'self-rupturing force': the unconscious (Mollow 2012: 287). 'Disableization' is that set of discursive operations by which 'the disabled' are made to embody the beyond of the normal (Tremain 2017: 96). Even 'benign' metaphors of disability imply a state of impairment that speaks for itself and can be used to figure other, more complex, states of being (Tremain 2017: 32–3); Bersani's shattering *jouissance*, for example, or the Lacanian ego. This is how disability has operated as the 'master trope of exclusion' in modernity (Snyder and Mitchell 2006: 125).

Anna Mollow calls it the 'disability drive'. Disability in our culture is abhorred and pitied, yes. But it is also *'fantasized'* in terms of a loss of control. Disability is 'both desired and feared' (Mollow 2012: 297). 'We desire what shatters us; we desire what disables us' (301). Joseph Valente explores that dynamic here, in response to Ato Quayson's (2010) influential reading of *Murphy*. For Valente, Quayson misreads the novel's 'autistic dynamic' in line with the character's fantasy of himself. Murphy *does* desire autistic isolation, but Beckett debunks this as ableist fantasy. We must distinguish between 'autistic desire' and Murphy's 'desire to be autistic'. Murphy is work shy. He despises capitalist relations and, in response, fetishes an autonomy that is always-already lost to the split subject of desire. Murphy's fond hope of autology, in this reading, is 'an underdetermined prompt to a desire that can never be realised'. In homage to Lacan, Valente calls it 'the *objet petit a(u)*'.

For Tim Dean, as Foucault (1990: 5), psychoanalysis has contributed, often unwittingly, to humanism's normalising project. Even Lacan's rebarbative return to Freud did not fully excavate its normative implications (Dean 2000: 247–53). All along, Lacan staked the integrity of his project on its critique of the normalising tendencies within psychoanalysis itself: ego psychology (1988), and object relations (1994). But it was not until the advent of the *objet petit a* – the metonymic object/cause of desire (Dean 2000: 250) – that he finally got there. *All* sexual identity is predicated on restriction, that is, fixation, and is perversely normalising. Dean dehumanises desire in ways that sit uncomfortably with liberal ideals of autonomy. He announces the 'death' of man as master of the world because master of himself (2000: 240–1). At its best, he suggests, psychoanalysis is not a humanism. In disability studies, too, Mollow, Tremain, Snyder and Mitchell all warn against any unthinking accommodation to the humanist project. Foucault was right to posit a causal link between human-ism and abnormalisation (Tremain 2017: 68). 'The human' has always been constituted by an 'arbitrary' line drawn between normal and abnormal (Snyder and Mitchell 2006: 128). To be deemed disabled is to be disqualified from humanity using largely aesthetic criteria (Siebers 2010; Snyder and Mitchell 2006: 122). Ableism is a beauty cult. The goal, therefore, is not to 'humanize the disabled', but to 'undo, or disable, the category of the human' (Mollow 2012: 308). The sense is that to 'be' beyond the normal we must move beyond 'the human'. Something similar had occurred to Beckett as he stumbled through the rubble of Saint-Lô. 'To find a form that accommodates the mess', he told Tom Driver as late as 1960: 'that is the task of the artist now' (Driver 1961: 218).

Chapter 1

Murphy and the Tao of Autism

Joseph Valente

My purpose is not to discover the presence of autism in Samuel Beckett's *Murphy*, but to bury its recent discovery in order to relocate autism as a magnetising and mobilising *absence* in the novel – not something that is lacking or deficient in itself, as the ableist constructions of autism propose, but a difference that is lacking, or better yet wanting, in the eponymous *non-autistic* protagonist and, by metaphorical extension, in neurotypical subjectivity as such. I denominate this lack, this want, the *objet petit a(u)*, with the translingual pun that entails on the Lacanian Other.

Autism has been excavated in *Murphy* by a leading neurodiversity scholar, Ato Quayson, known for coining the influential, usefully versatile concept 'aesthetic nervousness', in order to describe the disruptive impact that disability can have on the protocols of literary realism. In 'Autism, Narrative and Emotion' (Quayson 2010; hereafter Q), Quayson looks to extend its reach by isolating what he calls a generalised 'autistic dynamic' in the narrative (Q 839). But, as I will detail, his project hinges upon and is largely vitiated by a reliance on sloppy, outdated diagnostic markers of autism and their still more dubious application to the title character.

Autism is a profoundly heterogeneous syndrome, both qualitatively and in degree of severity, presenting in such a wide and fluctuating array of symptomatic combinations that each individual case represents not just an *instance* but a *variant* of the condition. The diversity of autistic manifestations beggars the metaphor designed to embrace them, the so-called autistic spectrum. Accordingly, to diagnose a literary character with autism, and particularly to do so in retrospect (*Murphy* predating the 'discovery' of autism by several years), ineluctably traffics in stereotypes that are based in yet diverge from reality, accurate yet fragmentary profiles, anecdotal exemplars, standing plausibly but imprecisely for a larger population. Of all the disability-based objects on offer in literary studies, autism allows for the greatest selectivity in the adducing, deployment and interpretation of behavioural or symptomatic evidence. For this reason, autism has proven especially liable to false (literary) positives, with neurotypical figures such as Darcy in *Pride and Prejudice*, intellectually disabled characters like Lenny in *Of Mice and Men*, or emotionally fragile figures like Laura in *The Glass Menagerie* all receiving spurious and misleading autistic diagnoses on differing grounds (e.g. Loftis 2017: 79–100). With this in mind, the emergent field of autism studies – the disciplinary provenance of my essay – must remain especially vigilant in upholding some benchmarks, however fuzzy or flexible, of controvertibility.

Quayson puts those limits and that vigilance to the test. They disavow any responsibility for 'tracking [. . .] discrete symptoms of autism' even as the 'autistic dynamic' he divines rests upon the 'features of autistic disorder' characterising 'the eponymous protagonist' (Q 840–2). That is to say, Quayson reserves the right to invoke stock characteristics of autism – and thus to 'safely assume' the autism of Murphy himself (Q 840) – without having to corroborate or validate their presence in the text. Treating these supposed features of autism under nebulous colloquial headings, the article inflates the stereotypes of the condition, ineluctable in any case, into full-blown caricatures, to be aligned by force with likewise mistaken estimates of Murphy's own psychosocial constitution. Thanks to the mostly deserved prestige of the author, however, the argument has garnered not just credibility but wide acceptance within the disability studies community. The dual effect, which I am hoping to offset, has been to sanction an already disturbing laxity in the autistic study of literature and to obscure the true autistic dynamic at work in *Murphy*, its proleptic endorsement of certain valorisations of autistic difference currently being fashioned within the neurodiversity movement.

The long dominant 'social first' nosology of autism, wherein the heart of the syndrome is taken to be a crippling incapacity or impairment in social intercourse (Schreibman 2005: 26–36), has defined the field from the beginning. The first detailed case study of autism also laid the foundation for the social first nosology in Kanner (1943). Quayson defines Murphy's place on the spectrum in terms of four different types or scales of self-enclosure, all of which are commutable with one another as metonyms of 'social isolation': mindblindness, silence, stillness and fascination with closed systems.

Mindblindness: To establish Murphy's autistic *bona fides*, Quayson diagnoses him with what the prominent cognitive psychologist

Simon Baron-Cohen (1995) denominates 'mindblindness', an inability to discern other people's intentions or even to attribute intentions to them. Once a widely-accepted reading of autism, theory of mind, of which mindblindness is a version, has steadily lost ground with the rise of neurosensory approaches to the syndrome, but remains pre-eminent in the field of cognitive psychology, and in the popular imagination (see Happé 1994: 34–51; Frith 2003: 77–97; Hobson 2002: 143–8; Ramachandran 2011: 136–52; Rozga et al. 2011; Frith and Happé 1999). Whatever the general validity of the postulate, Murphy's witty repartee with Neary, Celia, Ticklepenny and Bim clearly indicates that he suffers no deficiency in this regard. Far from countering this impression, Quayson's sole attempt to illustrate his ostensible mindblindness misconstrues the disorder itself, let alone its applicability to Murphy: '[Murphy] insists, for instance, on interpreting Celia's desire to 'make a man out of him' as something that will lead to their mutual destruction' (Q 845). Murphy's gloss on Celia's project does not even speak, in the first instance, to its animating intent, but rather to its likely ruinous consequences, about which Murphy actually proves quite prescient. At the same time, his foreknowledge of the cost of complying with Celia's wishes, that he will lose his mind and with it 'all', proceeds from a quite sophisticated apprehension of the ideological contours of Celia's intent or objective. He knows that the man Celia proposes to 'make out of him' does not follow some universal, ontological pattern, but rather embodies a specific historical norm, that of capitalist modernity, a *homo economicus* of a sort, someone whose very masculinity would be bound up with and evinced by his zealous capacity as a provider. Since Murphy has from the start of the novel recoiled from the practice of commercial exchange – 'the echo of ... quid pro quo! quid pro quo!' (M 1) – it is hardly surprising, and not at all mindblind of him to regard Celia's proposed marketplace of labour as a 'mercantile gehenna' or her productivist standards as a violation of the very terms of his being (M 25). But Murphy's discerning gaze into Celia's psychic impetus goes a level deeper still. He recognises that the instrumentalist norms to which she would assimilate him taint her very affection, rendering it 'love with a function' (M 23). Far from impaired, Murphy's theory of mind, at least when it comes to Celia, proves remarkably incisive.

Silence: Whatever speech, language and/or communication problems many autistics display, few are entirely *silent*, and the stereotypical profile of autism involves a good deal of paraverbal as well as verbal expression – groaning, humming, self-dialogue and, under duress, screaming and even barking (Wilson 2008: 35). Having said that, Quayson's attribution of this trait to the highly articulate Murphy seems even more gobsmackingly misbegotten. Quayson concedes that Murphy's silence must be understood figuratively (a badly mixed metaphor at best), as the practical effect of his elusive and enigmatic mode of verbal expression, which condemns him, on Quayson's view, to social isolation. Yet surely Murphy's purposeful verbal interactions with a host of characters – Neary, Miss Counihan, Vera the waitress, the medium Miss Dew, Ticklepenny and, for the most part, Celia – serve to belie this analysis altogether. Here again, Quayson offers but one illustration of Murphy's supposedly 'autistic' illegibility, and it tellingly involves his dissent from Celia's demand for remunerative labour, a quid pro quo for her amorous blandishments (Q 847). Of all Murphy's conversation with Celia, in fact, only his defence of his joblessness leaves her at a loss, and her very manner of describing the effect of Murphy's words – 'like difficult music heard for the first time' (M 25) – suggests that her puzzlement derives not from the incoherence of Murphy's discourse but from its musical fluency in advocating a position she finds incomprehensible, in the colloquial sense. The communication breakdown arises not from the 'aporetic' nature of Murphy's speech, as Quayson holds, but from the aporetic nature of his relationship with Celia. And far from being autistic, the latter aporia – comprising issues of love and work, sex and money – is typical, all too (neuro)typical.

Stillness: Stimming, pacing, seizures, agitation and, most pertinently for us, rocking – nothing is less characteristic of autistic subjectivity than stillness. If stillness is to be taken as a measure of autistic self-enclosure, as Quayson proposes, then autistic engagement with the environment must be accounted more robust than generally thought. Autism should never be confused with catatonia, as is sometimes still the case in popular renditions. By the same token, stillness cannot be thought an endemic trait of Murphy, whose perennial and perennially thwarted quest to find stillness confesses that he does not, until the time of his death, properly inhabit or enjoy it. To be sure, Murphy's chief self-pacifying measure, his rocking chair hobby, does bear an outward similarity to autistic habits of rocking in place and other paroxysmal activity associated with the syndrome. But whereas Murphy restrains his body to quicken his mind, an autistic typically vibrates his body to calm his mind. Rather than equating Murphy's practice with the autistic routine, any correlation of the two would necessarily harbour this reversal of aim or motive at its heart.

Fascination with closed systems: Quayson draws upon Baron-Cohen's later 'systematiser' theory of autism, which holds that subjects on the spectrum invest in abstract structures, regulated dynamics and orderly, impersonal mechanisms at the expense of empathic attachments and human bonds (Baron-Cohen 2003: 68–94, 133–54). Quayson judges Murphy, qua autist, to be 'generally unemotional' and condemned to 'tie his emotions exclusively to ordered patterns and systems' (Q 852, 860). This, the central plank in Quayson's brief, represents both a misapprehension of the systemiser thesis itself and a gross misreading of Murphy's affective disposition. With respect to the thesis, Quayson everywhere substitutes 'emotion' for 'empathy' and thereby mistakes the already invidious profile of autism as affiliative disorder for a much older, utterly discredited, empirically preposterous identification of autism with 'flat affect', an insensibility bordering on emotional catalepsis. As anyone who has experienced autism first-hand or has had sustained contact with autistics would surely attest, the syndrome tends to engender a different, unevenly ventilated, but if anything more vigorous capacity for affective response. And as anyone with a fine-grained familiarity with *Murphy* should recognise, neither of these autistic models pertains, with any exactitude, to the protagonist. Concerning Celia, in particular, Murphy finds his cherished, self-styled restraint and insouciance periodically countermanded by amorous and even empathetic feeling, in the absence of any systemic connection whatever. At one point, he expresses his sentiments in terms of rather clichéd (which is to say, neurotypical) romance: 'what is my life now but Celia' (M 11). Subsequently arguing over his job status, Murphy is 'carried away by his passion for Celia' (M 24), only to be 'left in the lurch by his emotion' later, upon finding her perversely indifferent to his having secured gainful employment at her command (M 84). Nevertheless, upon enacting his decision to quit Brewery Road, he evinces a notable degree of empathy for Celia's disappointment:

> He did not want her to feel, at least he did not want to be present when she felt, how far all her loving nagging had gone astray . . . how her efforts to make a man of him had made him more than ever Murphy. (M 114)

Warring against his contrary need for sequestration and solitude, Murphy's passion for Celia is imbued with more than a touch of ambivalence, but the resulting complexities of his inner life do not support, rather they scotch, the claim of his being 'generally unemotional' or apathetic. It is precisely the occasional puncturing of

Murphy's habitual, abstracted cool by surprisingly fervid feeling that helps to explain why Wylie's *sententia* summarising his attraction for women, 'his surgical quality', proves 'not *quite* the right word' (M 38, emphasis added).

While Quayson's reading tends to insist that 'his surgical quality' *is* 'quite the right word' for Murphy, as 'arguably autistic', he is in fact less concerned with this stereotypical bearing in its own right than as an effect of what he judges to be the 'hermetically sealed nature of Murphy's mind', a construct he treats as the novel's ultimate trope of 'social isolation' (Q 849). In other words, he borrows the systematiser profile of autism only insofar as it can be turned to the service of the 'social first' thesis. Thus, although computer circuitry and coding have over the last two decades emerged as a dominant model of mind in cognitive psychology and within the field of autism studies (Hayles 2005: 193–213), Quayson puts less of a premium on the internal systematicity of Murphy's mind and more on its detachment from and defence against its own outside, on its being, by Murphy's own lights, split off from both the embodied world and from any feeling not essentially cognitive in nature, hence from any possibility of social adhesion.

Quayson's delineation of 'Murphy's mind' not only encapsulates the general tenor of diagnosis, it also:

(a) reveals the perspective from which that autistic diagnosis could seem plausible, all evidence to the contrary; and in the process,
(b) reveals the way in which that diagnosis remains relevant to the reading of Murphy, despite being profoundly in error.

That is, Quayson's understanding of Murphy's mental landscape constitutes the juncture where the critic's measure of the protagonist converges with the *méconnaissance* or self-misrecognition of the protagonist himself, or rather the juncture where that convergence comes to the surface and becomes legible. To put it another way, Quayson misrepresents Murphy's mind out of an identification with Murphy's Imaginary self-conception, the viewpoint of his ego. What Quayson portrays is not, as he believes, how that mind 'really was' (M 65). Indeed, the text explicitly refuses such an accurate mental topology as 'an extravagance and an impertinence' (M 65), restricting itself to 'what [the mind] felt and pictured itself to be' (M 65). It is important in this regard to keep in mind that the entirety of chapter 6, the 'bulletin' mapping 'Murphy's mind', unfolds under the epigraph '*Amor intellectualis quo Murphy se ipsum amat*' (the intellectual love with which Murphy loves himself) (M 65; Ackerley 2010: 116). Quayson's account of the reality of Murphy's mind is thus predicated, as its only evidence and frame of reference, upon a deeply self-interested interior portrait. This epigraph indicates not only that the lineaments on offer of Murphy's mind are the projection of his narcissistic cathexis, his self-love or ego-eroticism, but that his auto-affection reduces to a love of his intellectual dimension or pretension. He loves, can only love, the abstracted, purely cognitive mask of himself that Quayson accepts as his truth.

Inconsistencies and self-contradictions pervade Murphy's extended self-reflection and they specifically serve to undermine his own preferred image of a 'hermetically sealed' citadel of thought. Indeed, the picture of a 'large hollow sphere' of mental abstraction is riddled from the start by references to the 'felt', to the emotions and sensations animating this 'sphere': 'solely with what it felt and pictured itself to be'; 'the mind felt its actual part to be above'; 'it felt no issue between its light and dark'; 'he felt his mind to be bodytight'; Murphy felt himself sovereign and free; 'choice of bliss' (M 65–8). The mind–body cognitive–affective split is thus destabilised in its very emergence. Further along, it is said that Murphy 'felt himself split in two, a body and a mind', even as he knew 'they had intercourse', a disavowal (I know it is so but . . .) which scrambles their respective functions (M 66). The ostensibly detached mind knows of the connectivity that feeling, the source of that connectivity, seems to deny. But, the passage continues, 'he [nevertheless] felt his mind to be bodytight and did not understand through what channel the intercourse was effected' (M 66). Here, the metaphor 'bodytight' sustains the deliberate confounding of the two dimensions or, if you prefer, confutes their partition. Its intended meaning, that he felt the mind tightly sealed as a distinct body, jostles with the punning connotation, that he felt his mind to be tight with his body, inseparable. Ultimately, 'Murphy was content to accept the congruence of the world of the body and the world of the mind or any other solution', for that matter, 'that did not clash with the feeling, growing stronger as Murphy grew older, that his mind was a closed system subject to no principle but its own, self-sufficient and impermeable to the vicissitudes of the body' (M 66). That is, he was content so long as the acknowledged congruence or tightness of mental life and bodily affect or sensation remained nugatory in effect, leaving the Imaginary of the detached or cloistered ego intact. Looking to dismiss this lexical challenge to Murphy's Cartesian fantasy, Quayson declares feeling in the text to be 'more cognitive than emotional . . . in accordance with the general attempt to objectively anatomize the mind' (Q 849). But as we have seen, the text openly forswears any attempt 'to objectively anatomize the mind' as 'an extravagance and an impertinence'. To this end, Beckett carefully distinguishes the meaning of the cognitive and the emotional in Murphy's failed attempt to segregate their psychic operation: 'He neither felt a kick because he thought one nor thought a kick because he felt one' (M 66).

Here, the text discloses the stark internal contradictions in Murphy's 'little world'-view, even as they are elided in Murphy's own (self-)consciousness. But more importantly than that, the text reveals this *méconnaissance* on Murphy's part to follow, as it must, in the paths of his desire. The 'feeling' of impregnable, systemic mindedness is shown to be not just the state of Murphy's apperception, but both the stuff of his contentment and the limit of his aspiration. At the very centre of Murphy's deliberations on what might be deemed (as Quayson does) the autistically abstracted, self-contained nature of 'Murphy's mind', hence at the very centre of Murphy's relationship to what might be deemed (as Quayson does) a certain dominant profile of autism, the question of desire asserts itself decisively.

As we noted at the start, the retrospective diagnosis of literary characters as developmentally disabled is not uncommon. Neither is an eagerness to allow the subject of such disability to speak for him- or herself and to credit the resulting testimony. Quayson might, at a stretch, be seen as adopting this strategy and taking it to the point of a full-blown transference. He identifies with and thereby replicates Murphy's apperception, mistaking it for the reality of Murphy's mind. But this apprehension, or misapprehension, in turn has its foundation in another, analogous deadfall of critical transference: Quayson identifies with and thereby replicates Murphy's *desire* for himself, mistaking it for the reality of Murphy's being-in-the-world. Quayson believes that Murphy fits an autistic profile, centred on social isolation, not on any reliable behavioural or symptomatic basis, but because in order to love himself, Murphy needs to imagine his mental domain in terms now associated with an autistic subject-position. But Murphy's self-styled distaste for modern, instrumentalised social relationships does not, cannot, stand as a warrant for Quayson's diagnosis, nor as evidence that Murphy displays the approved autistic markers of social deficit imputed to him. Taken from the medical model of autism, in both its cognitive and neuroscientific wings, those markers invariably speak to the issue of normative social *competency*, not normative social *investment*, to *deficiencies* in the rudimentary tools of social engagement (language, attention, reciprocity), not to *differences* in the readiness, willingness, or zeal to employ those tools.

Now, to be sure, certain cognitive and neuroscientists have advanced the thesis, curiously unremarked by Quayson, that autistic deficits in social competency can manifest in a lack of interest in interpersonal contact, a depressed motivation to participate in social interaction, and the experience of aversive effects from such participation: anxiety, distress, physical discomfort. Still, nothing about this amygdala-based thesis bears upon Murphy's idiosyncratic brand of sociality – his reluctantly engaged, equivocally accessible fetishism of inaccessibility and disengagement. Taken whole, in fact, the narrative shows Murphy is far from uniformly disinclined to social communication or emotional connection, as his relationships to Neary, to Celia, and to the inmates of Magdalen Mental Mercyseat all attest. Although he clearly internalises his mentor Neary's early judgement that his conarium (the Cartesian bridge between mind and world) has shrunk to nothing, even his most casual interaction, as with the waitress Vera, or the medium Miss Dew, demonstrates no affliction, no shrinking, from social contact. As 'seedy solipsists' go, Murphy is almost genial.

All of this is to say, Murphy is not a subject of autistic desire, as stereotypically defined by a congenital or constitutional proclivity for social detachment and remoteness. Rather, he is a subject who desires to *be* so autistic. As his mind-view indicates, his wish, echoed by Quayson, is to embody the asocial profile of autism and rest in that self-definition. But of course, desire bespeaks lack. His desire for a properly autistic structure of desire only goes to show that he does not possess or occupy said structure. His persistent wish to fit an asocial typology, most dramatically manifest in his identification with Mr Endon, only goes to show that he does not in fact belong. Why not? The reason is not far to seek. The word 'autism' derives from the word 'self', the primary denotation of which is having a single character or quality. The stereotype of the autistic subject as turned in upon the self, radically introverted, presupposes a singular, undivided subject, not, in Lacanian parlance, a subject of desire strictly speaking, but one of *jouissance*. By contrast, Murphy is a subject fully riven, a subject of psychomachia: one of its magnetic poles is a stereotypically autistic disposition towards segregation from the world, exemplified aptly by Murphy's rocking chair ritual; the other is the lure of social commerce and sexual intimacy, exemplified by his *pas de deux* with Celia. Murphy may have 'felt himself split in two, a body and a mind', but the split actually runs *within* his feelings themselves, within his libidinal make-up.

In this regard, Beckett seems to have taken Jean-Jacques Rousseau as a model for the character of Murphy. In 1934, shortly before he conceived *Murphy*, Beckett wrote to Thomas McGreevy to express his admiration for Rousseau as 'a champion of the right to be alone', and as an 'authentically tragic figure' in being frustrated in that right (LI 228). But he introduced a significant qualification as well. Rousseau was unfortunate in '*de ne pouvoir résister aux caresses*' (not being able to resist caresses) (LI 228). This summary judgement is no less germane to Murphy: 'If he could have known better how to trim his kite between the two positions, he would have suffered less' (M 123). Given the importance of the trimmed kite to Mr Willoughby Kelly, the bluff, unconflicted grandfather to whom Celia returns after Murphy's death, it would appear that Beckett was determined, at the unconscious as well as conscious level, to stake Murphy's subjectivity not on a cloistral autism but on a dualism, or more specifically, a dualism yearning after the cloisters of autism.

The fissured cathexis stirring Murphy to (in)action appears in the first pages of the novel, preparing us for what is to follow. The novel opens with Murphy in his rocking chair refuge from the cries of the marketplace, which herald the commodified practices of social interchange in the public sphere, Murphy's 'big world'. 'These were sights and sounds that he did not like. They detained him in the world to which they belonged, but not he, as he fondly hoped' (M 2). Notice that Murphy's 'autistic' disaffiliation from the social world exists in the realm of hope rather than fact, and of fond (foolish, naïve) hope at that. And so it proves to be. Murphy cannot refrain from inviting Celia to intrude upon his rocking chair retreat and to persuade him to ensure continued intimacy with her by agreeing to descend into the 'mercantile gehenna' in search of employment. (As a prostitute herself, Celia emblematises a cardinal property of the 'big world' that Murphy so regrets: the continuity, even inextricability, of the social and the commercial, the personal and the instrumental.) Not only does Murphy find himself torn between these inimical impulses of attachment and detachment, but the prepotency of the former, in defiance of any supposedly autistic tendency, sets the main action of the narrative in motion.

That being said, while Murphy's gravitation towards attachment proves stronger than his will to detachment on the plane of appetitive inclination – what Kant calls 'pathological' love – the magnetising appeal of the hermetically sealed 'little world' of the *autos* is decidedly more powerful at the meta level of moral judgement. Even as he beckons Celia to interrupt his reverie, we are told 'the part of him that he hated craved for Celia, the part that he loved shrivelled up at the thought of her' (M 5). This sentiment encapsulates Murphy's posture towards interpersonal sympathy generally and thus towards the autistic profile of 'social isolation'. His continued indulgence in the former precludes his assimilating to the latter, which unlike personal bonds, he can never possess, only pursue. If the two parts of Murphy, the appetitive (craving/shrivelling) and the attitudinal (self-loving/loathing), can be said to operate on different planes of consistency, their corresponding modes of partiality or preference occupy qualitatively different *dimensions*. The gamut of social interaction, from the 'music' of sexual congress with Celia – 'serenade, nocturne, and albada' (M 45) – to the marketplace sounds of commodity exchange, comprises positive objects of desire, whether affirmative or negative, while the state of radical, 'autistic' isolation and estrangement represents for Murphy an object/cause of desire, or *objet petit a(u)*, that is, an underdetermined prompt to a desire that can never be realised, let alone fulfilled on its own terms.

From the time of his removal to London, the prospect of Murphy's utter self-encasement exists strictly in relation to his abiding attraction to Celia – to be pursued in her advent as preparation, in her wake as resort, or in her presence as virtually shared ritual. Murphy is able to experience the *jouissance* of autistic dissociation – 'such pleasure that pleasure was not the word' (M 2) – but he is not able to *dwell* in it. Thus, 'I am not of the big world, I am of the little world was an old refrain with Murphy, and a conviction, two convictions, the negative first' (M 107). That it was a refrain, something that needs to be regularly repeated, consists with Murphy's oscillation between the two worlds, his belonging properly to neither. That Murphy needs to utter the refrain, to proclaim his posture at all, indicates that his intermittent residence in the little world signifies, and signifies primarily, his antagonistic relationship to the big, an inference corroborated in the passage itself, 'the negative [conviction] first'. Murphy exhibits the crucial distinction between social alienation, which always sustains an ongoing connection to the world spurned – and so is always also alienated from itself – and social isolation in the sense of a plenary 'autistic' abstraction or self-seclusion. Inasmuch as Murphy's schismatic desire articulates, however abrasively, the worlds or forms of habitus it would dissever, his commitment to and pursuit of isolation necessarily includes its more sociable other, cancelling itself out in this plenary autistic sense.

Murphy's unwonted eagerness to assume Ticklepenny's employment at Mercyseat may thus be understood dialectically. The post seems to offer him an opportunity to sublate his contradictory desires in favour of the 'little world', the autistic fortress of solitude. Once Murphy enters the institution, his oscillation between social adhesion and radical estrangement and self-enclosure resolves itself into a *single-minded identification* – hence psychosocial affiliation – with those already profoundly estranged and self-enclosed, in Murphy's phrase 'all those lives immured in mind' (M 108). That is to say, Murphy aims to fashion or find a positive object of desire that fully materialises, is flush with, the object/cause of his desire.

Beckett introduces a clever, allusive metaphor to illuminate the stakes of this quest. Instructing Murphy early on in the ways of Eros, Neary recalls William James's characterisation of neonatal experience: 'All life is figure and ground. The face . . . against the big blooming buzzing confusion. I think of Ms. Dwyer' (M 3; Ackerley 2010: 36). Neary's adaptation of James metonymises the beloved as a master signifier, the *point de capiton* (Lacan 1993: 268), focalising an otherwise amorphous, circumambient desire. At her first appearance, Murphy muses upon Celia in exactly the same phraseology: 'The beloved features emerging from the chaos were the face against the big blooming confusion of which Neary has spoken so highly' (M 19). The concentration of Celia's image, in turn, precipitates a moment of ardent emotional and erotic connection: 'He closed his eyes and opened his arms. She sank down athwart his chest' (M 19). Murphy finds in Celia an object of desire, and here 'pleasure' is indeed the word. Upon arriving at Mercyseat, however, he finds that his emulous attraction to Mr Endon cannot be so objectified. Rather, Endon appears as 'Neary's big blooming buzzing confusion mercifully free of figure' (M 147). Mr Endon, you see, successfully embodies a thoroughgoing removal from the Symbolic Order. Therefore, he remains 'free of figure', mobilising desire not as an object or signifier, in an economy of exchange and substitution, but as desire's indeterminate parasymbolic ground, the provenance of *objet petit a*. For this very reason, Murphy cannot take Endon on his own autistic terms, as the chess game featuring Endon's maddeningly self-recursive style of play is designed to illustrate. Endon's performance does not, as Quayson holds, 'replicate' Murphy's mind (Q 855), but eludes all reciprocal relation whatsoever. To engage Endon, as Murphy futilely attempts, would be to mitigate his defining asociality, to relocate him, however marginally, in the big world, towards which he is constitutively estranged. Murphy's idealisation of Endon as a model and a counterpart thus founders on a performative contradiction, violating the 'ground' of Endon's appeal in the very act of consecrating it.

By the same token, Murphy's effort at sublating his attachment–detachment conflict by affiliating himself with a monadic tribe meets insuperable internal obstacles. Newly vested, Murphy 'was anxious to test the striking impression that here was a race of people he had long since despaired of finding' (M 102). His sentiments, anxiety and despair, signal a need for kinship, a desperation for community, starkly at odds with the desideratum, the virtue, that Murphy looks to find in and with them. Murphy remains in denial concerning this self-contradiction: 'He would not have admitted that he needed a brotherhood'; but, the text proceeds to assure us, 'He did' (M 106). In a further twist of the dialectical screw, Murphy all but cognises that he needs this brotherhood as an inspiration to transcend *this very need*, to achieve plenary self-sequestration. 'What more vigorous fillip could be given to the wallows of one bogged in the big world than the example of life to all appearances inalienably realized in the little' (M 109).

None of this is to suggest that Murphy's extravagant identification with the 'cast off' inmates is without significant constructive effect. Beyond fostering his exceptionally respectful performance as an orderly, it affords him insights strikingly prophetic of twenty-first-century disability studies, including a critique of functionality, which Murphy deems 'duly revolting' (M 107), and of psychosocial normativity (the 'scientific conceptualism that makes contact with outer reality the index of mental well-being'; M 106). Finally, there is a remarkable anticipation of the contemporary clash between the social and the medical models of disability – here cast as the 'psychotic and psychiatric points of view' (M 100) – in which Murphy comes down decisively on the side of the former, with 'esteem for the patients and loathing of the textbook attitude towards them' (M 106). Indeed, Murphy proleptically articulates a credible summary of the social model as it pertains to autism and associated mental conditions: 'One had merely to ascribe their agitations, not to any flaw in their self-seclusion, but to its investment by the healers' (M 108), that is, the main challenges of their disability could be attributed not to the condition itself but to a hostile or unaccommodating therapeutic environment: 'Left in peace', Murphy opines, 'they would have been as happy as Larry' (M 108).

However, just as social alienation is not the affective equivalent of radical self-cloistering, so to express solidarity is not the social equivalent of belonging. In this case, it is just the opposite. Murphy's sense of solidarity with the inmates, his 'feelings of respect and unworthiness' (M 102), explicitly arises out of a wish for kindred on his part, a wish that Mr Endon and his fellows are constitutively undisposed to share. Murphy's longing to belong to *this* particular group is perhaps the surest sign that he doesn't. Murphy requires the gaze of another to witness his belonging to autistic otherness, and that gaze will only come from the normative or neurotypical 'big world'. That is why, during nightshift, when the absence of 'the adminicles' left him 'no loathing to love from', he has trouble 'imagining himself one of the patients'. 'There was nothing but he, the unintelligible gulf and they', a gulf he felt 'painfully' (M 143). That is also why Murphy's one triumphant moment experiencing a sense of belonging comes not in the company of the inmates, but of Ticklepenny, Murphy's predecessor: 'Murphy's night was good ... perhaps the best ... the self whom he loved had the aspect, even to Ticklepenny's inexpert eye, of a real alienation ... or conferred that aspect on the self he hated' (M 116).

Why does the 'aspect of a real alienation' accrue to the self whom Murphy hates rather than the self he loves? Because his alienation, however real, does not attain to the monadic quality of Murphy's ego ideal, the stereotypically autistic mind. Rather, it is itself an inevitably social product of a profoundly social – Hegel's primordially social – dynamic: the dialectics of recognition (Kojève 1969: 3–30), here enacted in visual terms between Ticklepenny's 'inexpert eye' and Murphy's mediated (all too mediated) self-regard. It is only by and upon stakeholders in the Symbolic, 'the big [Other]world', that such recognition might be conferred – by a Ticklepenny, who must extricate himself from Mercyseat, on pain of losing his mind, and upon a Murphy, who cannot completely extricate himself from the social covenant of quid pro quo in order to lose himself *in* his mind, like 'a mote in its absolute freedom' (M 68).

Beckett frames a deliberate contrast between this dialectics of recognition, featuring Ticklepenny's 'inexpert eye' on Murphy, and the scene precipitating Murphy's demise, wherein he 'brought Endon's eyes to bear on his, or rather his on them' (M 149), in the hope of forcing a dialectic gaze with an autistic savant or expert: the term 'autistic' was first used with reference to schizophrenics like Endon by Eugen Bleuler in 1911 (Evans 2013: 3). Murphy's earlier assumption that Endon had already 'recognized the feel of his friend's eye upon him' was previously debunked in the text, whose indirect free style suggests that the doubts belong to Murphy himself. In any event, its report captures perfectly the logic of Murphy's inevitable frustration:

> Mr. Endon would have been less than Mr. Endon if he had known what it was to have a friend, and Murphy more than Murphy if he had not hoped

against his better judgment that his feeling for Mr. Endon was in some small degree reciprocated. (M 144)

Given this passage, which epitomises the tenor of their rather brief cohabitation, it is difficult to see why Quayson could imagine that Endon 'replicated' the core properties of 'Murphy's mind'. To the contrary, it is in Murphy's nature to seek such mutuality with the autistic Other, to try and establish a paradoxical meeting of self-sequestered minds, while it is in Mr Endon's nature to abide co-presence without any such meeting, to engage, as his chess strategy exemplifies, in the preference for 'parallel play', now famously characteristic of autistic children.

In their final scene together, the abortive gaze of recognition is literalised as a blank mirroring of eyeballs. Mr Endon does not even see Murphy for looking at him: 'The last Murphy saw of Mr. Endon was Mr. Murphy unseen by Mr. Endon' (M 150). The reversibility of the syntax in this sentence counteracted by the semantic opposition (saw/unseen) figures diagrammatically the jamming of the dialectics of recognition by Endon's self-bounded autistic integrity. The text proceeds to translate the (non-)exchange in explicitly affective terms, highlighting that 'unintelligible gulf' between the modes of mindedness: 'the relation between Mr. Murphy and Mr. Endon could not have been better summed up than by the former sorrow at seeing himself in the latter's immunity from seeing anything but himself' (M 150). Far from a mutuality of gazes, the synergy of syntax and semantics in this sentence reinforces a rebound or recoil of gazes that is *itself* anything but mutual. The encounter thus dramatises an aporia, the one mode of interface that defeats Hegelian dialectic, the one mode that founds the deconstructive undoing of meaning as such, and the one mode that has its most prominent contemporary enactment in the face off of autism, radically conceived, and neurotypicality: that is, *the relation between relation and non-relation* (Derrida 1968). That aporetic (non-)relation is precisely what is encapsulated in the text's last judgement on this matter: 'Mr. Murphy is a speck in Mr. Endon's unseen' (M 150). Here, if you like, we have what Ato Quayson was looking for: the novel's 'autistic dynamic'.

After his final re-encounter with Mr Endon 'ends on' a mismatch of mind, Murphy goes running across the asylum grounds, strips off his clothes and tries to call to memory the images of his past intimates – friends, lovers, family members. His continued identification with the profound asociality of Endon seems to impede him, however, triggering an existential crisis. *Pace* Quayson, who finds Murphy's inability to visualise past associates a proof of his autistic isolation, his felt need to reconnect mentally with his people, ratcheted as it is to the point of absolute desperation, only confirms his conventionally neurotypical hunger for social connection. What drives this last bender is precisely the failure to establish that sort of connection with the personification of his autistic ideal and thus to sublate the conflict between his appetite for relationship (the object of his desire) and his exorbitant will to monadic sovereignty (the object/cause of his desire). Significantly, his resolution (an unwittingly deathbed resolution) to return to Brewery Road and Celia, to submit to 'what continued to dive him' (M 108), represents the last swing of the narrative pendulum, the surrender of a long-sought *jouissance* that confesses its glorious impossibility.

In the very first landmark life writing about autism, *The Siege*, Clara Claiborne Park likens her daughter's syndrome to being in nirvana, a blessed estate free of all recognisable desire. Yet she nonetheless finds her daughter's beatitude 'monstrous', as it prevents her from sharing with her family the trials and triumphs, purposes and struggles of everyday life (Park 1967: 90). As the title suggests, Park introduced in response what soon became the standard trope of autism, as a kind of cage or prison in which the subject lies trapped and from which she must be released. The massive popularity of *The Siege* indexes the appeal it made to a normative or neurotypical audience. Park's account also echoes Beckett's novel, but in reverse order, throwing into relief just how advanced from a disability studies perspective is the portrayal of the autistic profile we have been tracing here. Like Park, Beckett represents autism as appearing, to neurotypical eyes, like a species of nirvana, free of the sociosymbolic pressures of desire haunting neurotypical subjectivity, but for that very reason an object of desire as well to those who so conceive it. The trope of autism as a defended formation operates in *Murphy* too, but not in the clichéd sense of a prisonhouse; rather, as a 'sanctuary ... from a colossal fiasco' (M 107), and more than that, a citadel denying the normative other access to its secrets, its prerogatives, its difference, its dignity. As the debate rages today between those who advocate autism awareness, with an eye to amelioration (Park's explicit position in *The Siege*), and those who advocate autism acceptance as benign human variation (Quayson's implicit position in his reading of *Murphy*), Beckett had already proposed some eighty years ago the autistic difference as an impossible desideratum, akin to the 'lost object' of psychoanalysis, or what I began by calling *objet petit a(u)*. Most importantly, he observes that autistic subjects would be less than they are to forfeit all purchase upon this difference and we neurotypicals would be more than we are to leave them enjoy in peace.

Chapter 2

Narrating Disruption: Realist Fiction and The Politics of Form in *Watt*

William Davies

World War II and its aftermath was a defining period of Samuel Beckett's personal and creative life. When Beckett was awarded the Nobel Prize for Literature in 1969, Karl Ragnar Gierow in his ceremony speech situated Beckett as an author writing very much in the shadow of the war, and identified five works – *Watt*, *Molloy*, *Malone Dies*, *The Unnamable* and *Waiting for Godot* – that signified his importance as a writer of the post-war moment:

> The world around had [. . .] changed when Beckett came to write again after *Watt*. All the other works which made his name were written in the period 1945–49. The Second World War is their foundation; it was after this that his authorship achieved maturity and a message. But these works are not about the war itself, about life at the front, or in the French resistance movement (in which Beckett took an active part), but about what happened afterwards, when peace came and the curtain was rent from the unholiest of unholies to reveal the terrifying spectacle of the lengths to which man can go in inhuman degradation – whether ordered or driven by himself – and how much of such degradation man can survive. (Gierow 2007)

In Beckett studies, however, the prevailing perception, then and since, has been of an aesthetic sensibility 'out of time' (Morin 2017: 22), unconcerned with the trappings of history. Though this view has been challenged (Kennedy and Weiss 2009; Morin 2017; McNaughton 2018, among others), it is still common to read Beckett's war for its symbolic implications. For C. J. Ackerley and S. E. Gontarski, for example, war to Beckett is 'another example of the human predicament, an emblem of a ruined humanity' (2004: 626). For Gierow, by contrast, the war mattered for what it was, not what it represented, and he distinguished carefully between the war and its aftermath. James McNaughton (2018) includes *Watt* in his defining account of

Beckett's politics of aftermath (60–78), but, as Gierow notes, *Watt* was written during the war itself and does not fit this picture.

If *Watt* is, in some obvious sense, a war book, it is often read in eccentric relation to its historical context. Though the published text appears little involved with the particulars of the war, its explosion of reason and impenetrable formal 'strategies' are taken to reflect the chaos of the period. The common sense that Beckett's work is unavoidably historical, yet difficult to locate historically, appears amply confirmed by the peculiarity of *Watt*. This despite appearing to contain 'no trace' of the war itself (Pilling 1994: 35). In 1977, however, Beckett told Sighle Kennedy: 'it was an escape operation from the horrors of that hateful time. If they crept in it was in spite of me' (LIV 460). Recent developments have improved our understanding of *Watt* in this regard. Patrick Bixby (2009) and Seán Kennedy (2014a) revealed clear links between *Watt* and the Irish 'Big House' literary tradition, establishing Beckett's complex negotiation of the genre's political implications within the context of modern Ireland, and the discourse of Ascendency adopted by W. B. Yeats. For Bixby, *Watt* is a 'satirical novel that mimics the protocols of realist fiction in order to criticise the Big House as the heart of irrationality, chaos, and darkness' (2009: 133). This offers a lens through which to consider the novel in terms both of Ireland and the chaos that subsumed Europe. Anna Teekell reads *Watt* as 'a purgatorial allegory of neutral Ireland' in which Beckett is not so much '*anticipating* epistemological crisis as *enacting* it' (2016: 248, 249), a reading that owes much to McNaughton's examination of *Watt* in relation to Beckett's encounters with Nazi propaganda during his travels in Germany in 1936–7 (2018: 60–78).

McNaughton reads the novel as a sustained interrogation of Irish neutrality, of 'complacency, valorizing doing nothing' (78). He also reads its formal experimentation as Beckett's exploration of the logic and processes of propaganda as he witnessed them (in very different forms) in Nazi Germany and the Irish Free State. In this view, we must look to Beckett's encounters with Nazi propaganda to account for the novel's experimentalism (2018: 61). However, when Beckett turned to formal experimentation as a method of composition for *Watt*, he was also enacting a critique of realist narrative fiction developed at Trinity College over a decade earlier. In this essay, I complicate McNaughton's account, recalling Bixby's characterisation of *Watt* as a satire of realist fiction, and situating the novel in relation to Beckett's *Dream of Fair to Middling Women* (1992; hereafter *Dream*, cited as D) and his lectures at Trinity College, Dublin.

Paul Sheehan argues that narrative is 'a uniquely human way of making order and meaning out of the raw material of existence', one which functions through 'the relation of time, meaning and language' (2002: 9–10). Such a conception of narrative draws the writing of fiction and the writing of history into close proximity. Various theorists have described the shared narrative structures of fiction and history. For Paul Ricoeur, 'history, in all its forms, even the most structural, even the least factual, falls under storytelling' (trans. in Carrard 2001: 467). Hayden White, meanwhile, argues that narrative involves 'the impulse to moralize reality' and is ubiquitous in both history and fiction, particularly the novel (1980: 23). For Roland Barthes, narrative is universal: 'present in every age, in every place, in every society. [. . .] It] is simply there like life itself' (1977c: 79). Shoshana Felman develops these insights in the context of World War II, arguing that conventional distinctions between history (as discipline) and narrative (as a 'mode of discourse and as a literary genre') were undermined by fascist propaganda (1992: 93). Felman claims, too, that the structures of propaganda in fascism complicate any universal, even optimistic, theories of narrative put forward by theorists like Barthes. Drawing on Barbara Herrnstein Smith's formulation of narrative – as 'verbal acts consisting of *someone telling someone else that something happened*' (in Felman 1992: 93) – Felman suggests that the connection between history and narrative is itself historically contingent, a prospect which was knowingly exploited in Nazism when the regime's extermination policies became reality (94).

As McNaughton attests, Beckett's 'German Diaries' reveal that he had realised the political implications of narrative's role in historical writing before the war had even begun. After reading Friedrich Stieve's pro-Nazi history of Germany, *Abriss der deutschen Geschichte von 1792–1935*, Beckett recorded his frustration with a narrative that conceives of Hitler's regime as the inevitable outcome of the nation's history (McNaughton 2018: 69). He was sickened by Stieve's revisionist storytelling. He realised that he couldn't 'read history like a novel' and concluded in his diary:

> I am not interested in a 'unification' of the historical chaos any more than I am in the 'clarification' of the individual chaos, & still less in the anthropomorphisation of the inhuman necessities that provoke the chaos [. . .;] the expressions 'historical necessity' & 'Germanic destiny' start the vomit moving upwards. (15 January 1937, in Nixon 2011: 87, 177–8)

Revisionists like Stieve would prove key to the legitimisation of the Nazi regime (Koonz 2003: 205). Major events in the development of the Nazi party, such as Hitler's elevation to chancellor on 30 January 1933, were recast as the inevitable culmination of modern European history (Koonz 2003: 10). In the case of the political conceptualisation of 'destiny' found in Nazi ideology, such narratives implied the necessity for violence and exclusion, the darker aspect of White's 'impulse to moralize' (1980: 23). It was this rhetoric, of a nation succumbing to intoxicating narratives of race and progress, that Beckett reacted against in his condemnation of Stieve's historical 'novel' of the German people.

McNaughton shows how the propagandist imprinting of 'Germanic destiny' onto history was, for Beckett, a worship of cause-and-effect that 'provoked' him 'to investigate how an experimental aesthetic might respond better than documentary realism to such a dangerous political ideology' (2018: 69). The result, McNaughton argues, is *Watt*. However, while the trip to Nazi Germany clarified the political stakes of Beckett's aesthetic concerns, distrust of historical narratives had informed his earlier dismissal of artistic realism and his experimentation with the novel form in *Dream*. With its linguistic play and disordered form, *Watt* exploits the 'human' dimension of narrative to explore the 'inhuman' potential of narrative, troubling the presumption that narrative entails 'order and meaning', let alone a moral impulse (Sheehan 2002: 10). *Watt*'s formal elements – disordered chapters, fragmentary 'Addenda', its attempt at 'recapturing, at will, modes of feeling peculiar to a certain time' (Beckett 2009b: 62; hereafter W) – combine to disrupt the normative expectations of the novel. *Watt*'s radical affront to the novel form is not only a parody of the propaganda which brought about the turmoil of the war but also a thoroughgoing interrogation of the norms of narrative form which Beckett critiqued across the 1930s, from his first novel *Dream* to his 'German Diaries'.

Early in his career, Beckett rejected what he saw as the artificial narrative cohesion of realist fiction writers such as Charles Dickens, Jane Austen, Thomas Hardy and, above all, Honoré de Balzac, author of *La Comédie humaine*. These were novelists who failed to 'preserve the integrity of incoherence' (Bolin 2013: 15). Hardy relies excessively on artificial coincidence (Ackerley and Gontarski 2004: 246). Dickens and Balzac are dismissed as 'Old Curiosities' (D 118), a conflation of Dickens's *The Old Curiosity Shop* (1841) and Balzac's *Le Cabinet des antiques* [*The Collection of Antiques*] (1822), which

Beckett read at Trinity (Pilling 1998: 15). Austen – 'the divine Jane' – and Balzac are decried as the authors of characters based on 'all falsity' (D 119) which present a 'deformation of life' (de la Durantaye 2016: 24). Beckett's dislike of Balzac was most sustained. In 1935, he could not decide, after reading *La Cousine Bette* (1846), whether the author was 'writing seriously or in parody' (LI 245; de la Durantaye 2016: 23). For Beckett, Balzac was the most egregious pedlar of 'the grotesque fallacy of a realistic art' (1999: 76), because he claimed to depict the comedy of human existence in its totality (de la Durantaye 2016: 21–5).

Balzac's currency in modern European culture, and Beckett's distrust of the author's presence in that culture, was in part bound up in the political philosophy derived from his work. W. B. Yeats was a particular champion of Balzac's literary and political values throughout his career, and he returned to Balzac with keen interest in the 1930s, a period in which Beckett had developed a powerful animosity towards Yeats's cultural politics, as professed in essays, letters and a now lost, unpublished review of Yeats's *Oxford Book of Modern Verse* for the *Irish Times* (Morin 2014: 214). For Yeats, Balzac's aristocratic sympathies, his belief in the 'suppression of the individual', had intense appeal (Stanfield 1988: 112–44; Howes 1996: 111). Yeats invoked Balzac often in his writings on the family, suggesting that Ireland might 'hammer its thought into unity' by giving Irish writers Balzac's fifty-volume *Comédie humaine* (Stanfield 1988: 114). The novel Beckett endured at Trinity, *Le Cabinet des antiques*, is pertinent: a cautionary tale of provincial noble houses brought down by the French Revolution. Wary of the rhetoric of revolution, Yeats found in Balzac a clarion call for those of noble blood to resist class upheaval; indeed, Yeats identified Balzac as a culture cure to the rumblings of Marxist revolution in early twentieth-century Ireland (Stanfield 1988: 114). The French Revolution also represented the wrong kind of revolution to Nazi ideology in the 1930s, and Nazi historians – including Stieve – reworked historical narratives to supplant 1789 with Hitler's rise to power in 1933 as the shaping force of modern Europe (Koonz 2003: 205). A year prior to his visit to Germany, Beckett took notes from various works on the French Revolution, notably George Peabody Gooch's *Germany and the French Revolution*, an analysis of the impact of the French Revolution on German cultural and social development (Knowlson 1996: 216, 746).

Yeats also incorporates Balzac's philosophy of race and revolution into essays such as 'Louis Lambert' (1934) (Howes 1996: 162). The same year, Beckett published 'Recent Irish Poetry', in which he critiques Yeats for his influence on modern Irish poetics, and the review 'Proust in Pieces' in which he laments the readers of Proust who 'cry for the sweet reasonableness of plane psychology à la Balzac for the narrational trajectory that is more like a respectable parabola and less like the chart of an ague' (Beckett 1983: 64). Yeats's narratives of nation and Balzac's 'plane psychology' alike drew Beckett's ire in 1934, just when Yeats was looking to Balzac to justify his increasingly anti-democratic views. In 'Louis Lambert', Yeats discusses Balzac's depiction of the French Revolution as the 'individual man armed with Liberty, Equality, Fraternity' pitted against families preserved by 'privilege, pride, [and] the rights of property', with both Balzac and Yeats siding with the latter (1961: 444). This echoes how the very phrase of the Revolution – '*Liberté, égalité, fraternité*' – came under attack during the war, and was replaced by Vichy with '*Travail, famille, patrie*', signalling the transformation through the regime's war-time *Révolution nationale* of individuals into collectives defined by a vision of 'true' France (Gibson 2010a; Davies forthcoming).

While it is likely Beckett would have found little redeeming value in Balzac's politics, he most directly lambasts the author for the narrative structure which unifies *La Comédie humaine*. In *Dream*, we find a proto version of the vocabulary of narrative 'anthropomorphism' used by Beckett in the 'German Diaries', here positioned in terms of writing 'human' life:

> To read Balzac is to receive the impression of a chloroformed world. He is absolute master of his material, he can do what he likes with it, he can foresee and calculate its least vicissitude, he can write the end of his book before he has finished the first paragraph, because he has turned all his creatures into clockwork cabbages and can rely on their staying put wherever needed or staying going at whatever speed in whatever direction he chooses. The whole thing, from beginning to end, takes place in a spellbound backwash. We all love and lick up Balzac, we lap it up and say it's wonderful, but why call it a distillation of Euclid and Perrault *Scenes from life*? Why *human* comedy? (D 119–20)

The narrator laments that the novel – and Belacqua, whose 'synthesis' is so intimately tied to the novel's structure (D 119) – does not even have 'a single Chesnel in [its] whole bag of tricks' (D 118), no sage old steward 'calculate[d]' (D 119) to rescue the novel and its central character. The '*human*' aspect of Balzacian fiction that Beckett rejects is also at the heart of his aversion to realist painting, which he describes with a similar language of 'anthropomorphism' in letters to Thomas McGreevy in 1934 and 1938 (LI 222–3, 598–9), letters which reveal the 'full-blown anti-humanism' to which he gravitated in the mid-1930s (Carville 2018: 86). In all the forms that Beckett aligns with a humanist perspective – realist writing, realist painting and historical writing – he identifies a structural 'anthropomorphism', the depiction of reality with a certain conception of the human at its core, later condemned in Watt's 'anthropomorphic insolence' (W 175).

Beckett's attacks on realist fiction in *Dream* signify his distrust of the conventions of narrative fiction. Balzac's 'chloroformed world' is one that Beckett, via *Dream*, can only designate as a falsehood, as literary artifice that closes down any representation of the irrational and contingent aspects of human life. Ending with an 'AND' (D 239) and an artificial 'End' in which Belacqua is simply asked to 'move on' (D 241), *Dream* is best conceived as a stunted *Bildungsroman* (Sugimoto 2017), the novel form which contributes most readily to the assumption that 'subjectivity is narrative-shaped' (Sheehan 2002: 135). For Beckett, though, such an assumption rests on the insincerity inherent in the implications of 'realist' writing. 'In Balzac', he told his students at Trinity College in 1930, 'all reality is a determined, statistical entity, distorted, with total reality not respected' (in Le Juez 2009: 26). Balzac's claim to depict 'the human condition', 'you may be certain that this drama is neither fiction nor romance. *All is true*' (Balzac 1951: epigraph), was the very thing that Beckett rejected (Le Juez 2009: 28). For Beckett, this is a falsification in which life is marshalled into strict, pre-ordained forms that dictate every outcome and value for each character or moment. It is this marshalling, this constraining of life to rationalised strictures, that Beckett identified too in the propaganda of Nazism. He saw that, in certain political conditions, the narrative politics of realist fiction lie also at the root of violent, exclusionary modes of identity essentialism.

Beckett's attacks on Balzac in *Dream* and his Trinity lectures contrast with the writing he favoured, namely Joyce, Proust and, above all during the Trinity lectures, Gide (Bolin 2013: 8), all of whom Beckett declared 'the successors of Dostoevsky [and so of the modern novel] because they dare to preserve the complexity of the real, the inexplicable, unforeseeable quality of the human being' (in Le Juez 2009: 29). In the 'German Diaries', this contention is reformed in political terms when Beckett expresses his desire to resist the rationalising 'unification' and 'anthropomorphisation' of history that he saw at work in Nazi propaganda's strategies of revising national narratives which put Nazism at the centre of German progress. The relation between historical and fictional narratives is never far apart for Beckett, though, and he returned to the issue of *narrative* progress in a 'German Diaries' entry dated 26 March 1937. Recording his conversation with Kurt Eggers-Kestner in Munich, Beckett reflects on the implications of Joyce's developments in the novel:

> The dissonance that has become principle & that the word cannot express, because literature can no more escape from chronologies to simultaneities, from nebeneinander [sequential] to miteinander [simultaneous], that the human voice can sing chords. As I talk & listen realise suddenly how <u>Work in Progress</u> is the only possible development from <u>Ulysses</u>, the heroic attempt to make literature accomplish what belongs to music – the miteinander & the simultaneous. Ulysses falsifies the unconscious, or the 'monologue intérieur', in so far as it is obliged to express it as a teleology. (26 March 1937, in Nixon 2011: 167)

Beckett's reflections on the limits of a Joycean 'teleology' echo his critiques of Balzac's 'narrational trajectory', revealing how his responses to the political narratives active in Nazi Germany at the time coincided with, even develop out of, a nearly decade-long negotiation of what Beckett saw as the fundamental problems of narrative falsification inherent to the novel tradition. However, it was not until *Watt*, amid the chaos of the war, that Beckett realised a creative form that synthesised his thinking on the aesthetic and political potential of narrative disruption.

The novel's manuscripts show that when Beckett commenced in 1941 what would become *Watt*, he began with a parody of the Big House literary tradition that satirises the fantasy of progress inherent to Balzac's and Yeats's vision of the family through the depiction of an Anglo-Irish aristocracy household in decline and degeneration, a process which exposes the 'irrational heart' of the shared tenets of Balzacian society, Yeatsian Ascendency and European fascism: 'domination underwritten by racialised claims of superiority' (Kennedy 2014a: 232). As Beckett developed the text through the war, formal experimentations in structure and language came to govern the delivery of this Big House satire. As a result, in the published text, the narrative form of Beckett's novel – one that resists 'the vulgarity of a plausible concatenation' (Beckett 1999: 81–2) – not only takes to task the 'irrational heart' of the Big House of Mr Knott but dismantles the narrative structures of progress and 'trajectory' (Beckett 1983: 64) which, according to figures like Yeats, instilled political necessity into the philosophy of family and the nation that Balzac advocated and which was at the heart of Vichy's wartime rhetoric.

Expanding the parody of the *Bildungsroman* begun in *Dream*, the published *Watt* explodes conventional narrative form, dictated as it is by 'the order in which Watt told his story' (W 186) and the relationship between Watt and his narrator, Sam, who attempts as best he can to record the story told him by Watt in the institution in which they both reside. While both the novel's title and, more importantly, Sam's presence with his 'little notebook' (W 108) suggest that the text will chart the life of a person named Watt, the text instead enacts through the misaligning of chapter order and chronology the disorientation of Watt's failure to impose logic or reason on his experiences. Diverting from the expected linear structure of a novel – beginning–middle–end – to one that is paratactical and discordant, what Beckett called 'the miteinander & the simultaneous', *Watt* bewilders the reader through Sam's attempts to remain faithful to his subject's mode of communication: 'As Watt told the beginning of his story, not first, but second, so not fourth, but third, now he told its end. Two, one, four, three, that was the order in which Watt told his story' (W 186). The novel reflects what Bob Perelman calls the 'the dominant mode of postindustrial existence': the parataxis of modernity in which life is defined by 'atomized' experiences rather than extended narratives (1993: 313). Conor Carville uses these same terms to describe the movement Beckett makes away from the 'flux' of *Dream* towards an aesthetics of incoherence and 'atomization' (2018: 86), one which becomes notably visible in the 'great formal brilliance and indeterminable purport' of *Watt* (W 61).

Several instances in *Watt* indicate that the familiar trappings of narrative are themselves in question. This is most apparent once Sam reveals that the novel is governed by what he has managed to record. Blurring the line between story and storyteller, between actor in the story and architect of its form and content, Sam describes the difficulties of narrative construction based on Watt's communications, asserting his role as both narrator of the text and chronicler of Watt's experiences:

For when Watt at last spoke of this time, it was a time long past, and of which his recollections were, in a sense, perhaps less clear than he would have wished, though too clear for his liking, in another. Add to this the notorious difficulty of recapturing, at will, modes of feeling peculiar to a certain time, and to a certain place, and perhaps also to a certain state of the health, when the time is past, and the place left, and the body struggling with quite a new situation. Add to this the obscurity of Watt's communications, the rapidity of his utterance and the eccentricities of his syntax, as elsewhere recorded. Add to this the material conditions in which these communications were made. Add to this the scant aptitude to receive of him to whom they were proposed. Add to this the scant aptitude to give of him to whom they were committed. And some idea will perhaps be obtained of the difficulties experienced in formulating, not only such matters as those here in question, but the entire body of Watt's experience, from the moment of his entering Mr Knott's establishment to the moment of his leaving it. (W 62)

Sam's problems converge around his own abilities as narrator-chronicler 'to receive' the information from Watt, the mode and contextual conditions in which Watt makes his 'communications', and the desire to 'recaptur[e]' and 'formulat[e]' the experiences described by Watt in a form that is both coherent and faithful to the events as Watt recounts them. Recalling the very problem that historical fact is dependent on narrative forms and conventions, as raised by Felman and others, Sam struggles with 'recapturing, at will, modes of feeling peculiar to a certain time' and is forced to give in to narrative impulses and interventions which ultimately undermine his stated goal. As such, the text parodies the very elements of what Beckett saw in both the German history text of Stieve and in the writing of Balzac: the attempt to 'rationalise' the fundamentally incoherent, 'inhuman chaos' of reality. The implications of the reported nature of the text are felt throughout as the novel humorously trades on the inconsistencies and even erroneous nature of a text based on unstable narrative foundations. The fictionalisation of the novel's materiality – '(Hiatus in MS)' (W 207) – and use of footnotes, for example, thwart the reliability of the main body of the prose. The Lynch family tree is recorded mathematically – 'Five generations, twenty-eight souls, nine hundred and eighty years, such was the proud record of the Lynch family, when Watt entered Mr Knott's service' – only to have a footnote inform the reader that 'The figures given here are incorrect. The consequent calculations are therefore doubly erroneous' (W 87). '[T]he obscurity of Watt's communications' seems to be the cause here and, in this instance at least, Sam, as narrator, is able to intervene. Yet, this introduces two problems. First, that Sam has caught this error but may have missed others due to his own limitations as chronicler. Second, a more pernicious prospect emerges with the revelation that Sam can edit and 'correct' Watt's testimony. The question becomes not just 'what kind of witness was Watt?' (W 175) but what kind of chronicler is Sam, and by what framework does he adjust and shape Watt's account?

The 'material conditions in which these communications were made' are also reported to have encroached on the novel's 'Addenda', blurring the division between narrator and author as a footnote suggests that 'only fatigue and disgust prevented [the] incorporation' of the present material (W 215). The contents of the 'Addenda' are at once implied to be fragments of the text which Beckett the author did not include (which they are), and fragments which Sam the narrator could not, or chose not to, place in the main narrative; indeed, some notes openly propose alterations that could undermine the whole narrative that precedes the 'Addenda': 'change all the names', for example (W 222). In so doing, *Watt* produces an engagement with the novel as a formal construct, as a container of narrative and (with particular pertinence to historical narratives presented as historical fact) the ways that narratives can be manipulated 'even when one is most careful to note down all at the time, in one's little notebook' (W 108). Together, the text's form and content evince a concerted interrogation of the construction and constructiveness of narrative, playing with the absurdity and artificiality that Beckett saw at work in the 'Germanic destiny' rhetoric of Nazism and the 'snowball effect' of realist fiction. As such, the 'nothingness' at the heart of Watt's own absurd process of logical abstraction and hyper-rationalisation in Mr Knott's house is also inscribed into any promise of narrative coherence or character development that the novel form conventionally suggests:

> What had he learnt? Nothing.
> What did he know of Mr Knott? Nothing.
> Of his anxiety to improve, of his anxiety to understand, of his anxiety to get well, what remained? Nothing. (W 127)

Such passages read as direct commentaries on the expectations of the novel produced by the realist and *Bildungsroman* tradition; the promise of self-improvement inherent in the *Bildungsroman* is replaced with the condemnation of Watt for his desire to rationalise his experience, and the anticipated structure of the novel is replaced with a nightmarish collapse of time and space that vitiates all progress, that most cherished of 'Enlightenment values' (Bixby 2009: 133).

In these terms, *Watt* gains political significance precisely because of the very structures of narrative that both its form and content work ceaselessly to complicate. Felman (1992) emphasises that this type of affront to narrative coherence in texts written in proximity to the war is a recognition of the moral implications of the global conflict itself and how 'traditional relationships of narrative to history' were violently destabilised by its horrors (1992: 95). In *Watt*, it is the novel's form which bears witness, not only in the performance of propaganda methods (McNaughton 2018), but in its paratactical form. We see in *Watt* not necessarily the direct representation of history itself – of the war, or even of a coherent picture of modern Ireland – but an engagement with the base function of narrative that history and fiction conventionally share. McNaughton suggests, via Barthes, that *Watt* 'shows' the 'process' of myth, whereby, in Barthes's formulation, meaning and form play off one another (2018: 63). Watt attempts to overcome the 'myth' of Mr Knott's domain, to get his facts straight, his house in order, as it were, yet is subsumed by linguistic and narrative collapse, the former a result of his experience working for Mr Knott, the latter a result of the collision between Watt's retelling to Sam and Sam's attempt to record Watt's account. Such a collapse makes apparent the various issues that orbit the desire to create and maintain a narrative based on the reportage of events or experiences, a desire which, to recall White, invariably involves an 'impulse to moralize' (1980: 23). However, as the propaganda of the 1930s and the horrors of the war revealed, this 'impulse' and the 'morals' themselves are contingent upon the political force enacting them. For Beckett, this was made most apparent in the propaganda of mid-century fascism, in the rhetoric of Nazism in which the 'impulse to moralize' was the impulse to mobilise myths of race and nation, and in the wartime propaganda of Vichy France in which the 'true' France was envisioned through narratives of peasant domesticity, the sanctity of the family, and unyielding patriotism (Gibson 2015; Davies forthcoming). Thus, the formal experimentation of *Watt* acquires its political charge most readily from Beckett's encounters with the propaganda techniques of these regimes, and of the Irish Free State too, as McNaughton argues (2018) – though some nuance is necessary when the charge of fascism is present in the context of Free State Ireland. Yet, the 'impulse' to disrupt conventions of form stems from Beckett's earlier work in *Dream* and from his thinking on realist fiction, meaning that we can trace how Beckett's aesthetic sensibilities shape his responses to the political ideologies he encountered.

With this in mind, we can read *Watt*'s structural elements as subverting not only the conventions of narrative in realist fiction, but also the penchant for narratives of progress dominant in political and national discourses that rely on central principles of 'necessity', 'trajectory' and 'destiny' within their frameworks of power. By no means rejecting the existence of an objective, factual or historical reality, for this is the very thing with which Watt attempts to engage in his 'anthropomorphic insolence', the novel nevertheless parodies both Watt's desire for coherence and logic and the expectation of structural coherence that the novel form implies.

Watt's attention to 'the notorious difficulty of recapturing, at will, modes of feeling peculiar to a certain time' reflects the historical and political conditions of its composition and the modes of political writing and propaganda that brought the 'vomit' upwards in Beckett. Sam makes clear this problem repeatedly when he acknowledges 'the difficulties experienced in formulating' his narrative of Watt due to the various issues of contextual conditions and communication (in particular, Watt's method of speech). In producing such a narrative conceit, the nature of the novel as a report or chronicle is revealed to also govern Watt's own existence. Watt fades in and out of the novel's partially formed reality as his movements to, from and between Mr Knott's house are variously accounted for by Sam. The construction of Watt's identity and experiences are possible only through Sam's retelling, a system that produces the ambiguous, even frustrating appearance and disappearance of Watt at the beginning and end of the novel; Watt disappears out of view amidst the conversations of Goff, Mr Hackett and Tetty, becoming 'a solitary figure, lit less and less by the receding lights, until it was scarcely to be distinguished from the dim wall behind it' (W 11).

What Beckett termed the 'narrational trajectory [. . .] à la Balzac' (1983: 64) is entirely bankrupted in *Watt* as the very desire for narrative is parodied. The sense that 'something happened' or of 'someone telling someone else that something happened' is consistently marred by the various logic games, absurd descriptions and formal idiosyncrasies in which the novel playfully indulges. Beckett makes central to the text the prospect of narrative disorder, encapsulated in its non-linear chapter structure and 'Addenda', and Sam's attempt to recount Watt's story in the manner in which it is reported. The text's status as an account created in the 'the order in which Watt told his story' emphasises that the text's structure is meaningful only to its source, and that the experiences (or 'facts') of Watt's entry into Mr Knott's house that the novel supposedly records are subject to the narrative in which they are contained. If Beckett found that the Nazi propaganda of German history demonstrated that he could not 'read history like a novel', and found such a prospect intellectually, perhaps even ethically, reprehensible, the narrative collapse of *Watt* confronts the very prospect and expectations of what is implied when one attempts to 'read [...] a novel' at all. Given the importance of particular narratives of nation and history that dominated the propaganda of the war and the events that preceded it, Beckett's wartime composition of a text in which narrative itself is a central theme produces a politics of form that at once highlights the very artifice that Beckett condemned in realist fiction and nationalist propaganda alike, and embraces in the absurdity made available by collapsing the expected stability and coherence that the novel form traditionally entails.

Chapter 3

'no human shape': Unformed Life in *The Unnamable*

Byron Heffer

What is the value of 'life' in Beckett's fiction? To be sure, the antivital – and its ironic offspring: the anti-natal – is an especially fecund theme in Beckett's work, endlessly reiterated in paradoxes and oxymorons. And yet as Andrew Gibson reminds us in his discussion of Beckett's anti-life sentiments: 'There have been many life-haters. But since they have known life only in and as particular historical occasions, they have always hated particular historical versions of life, even when they have asserted the opposite' (2010a: 16). This chapter enquires into the ways in which Beckett's encounters with the Nazi politics of life informed his presentation of the 'misshapen' body. Situating Beckett's post-war fiction in relation to Nationalist Socialist theories of art and eugenics, I argue that his incorporation of deformity contests the biopolitical paradigm in which aesthetic form gives value to life. While Hitler wanted to impose classical form on the German people by surgically removing degenerate flesh from the 'Aryan' body, Beckett distorts aesthetic form by incorporating disfigured flesh into his late modernist writing.

Arguably, Beckett was literary modernism's consummate maestro in the art of degeneration. The reasons why degeneration is a pervasive feature of his work are multiple and complex, yet it is possible to trace his fascination with the subject to close scrutiny of a single text. As John Pilling's edition of the '*Dream* Notebook' shows, Beckett studied Max Nordau's *Degeneration* (1892) in the early 1930s (1999: xvii). In this diatribe against symbolism and aesthetic decadence, Nordau claimed that the cultural forms of *fin-de-siècle* Europe were symptoms of an epidemic of physical and mental disorder which had its source in the biological decline of the species. Siobhán Purcell has explored the formative influence of his ideas on Beckett's representation of disability in his early fiction, arguing where 'Nordau lamented the perceived decline of physical and aesthetic form, Beckett privileges

[. . .] impaired states, even manifesting them at the level of form' (2015: 31). Further, Purcell argues that Beckett's 'concern with the conflated representation of aesthetic and physical form' testifies to his 'fascination with the nature of corporeal difference and a concomitant mission to deform his own work' (30). While I agree that notions of bodily deformity are key to Beckett's remaking of the novel form, Purcell does not take into account Beckett's negotiation with the biopolitical imperatives of early twentieth-century Europe. According to Joseph Valente, 'The image of disability in modernist literature is a highly-mediated effect of the development of the regime of biopower over the course of the nineteenth century' (2013: 380). My reading of *The Unnamable* suggests that Beckett's experiments with ideas of bodily and aesthetic deformity constitute a significant chapter in the history of this antagonism between modernism and biopolitics.

Let me pause here to offer a brief definition of biopolitics. Michel Foucault famously claims that the 'threshold of modernity' was reached 'when the life of the species is wagered on its own political strategies' (1998: 143). Once the life of the human species moves 'into the realm of explicit calculations', politics concerns itself with managing and optimising the health of populations (143). It is within this context that a normative conception of the human species becomes a defining element in the exercise of State power. As Foucault puts it, 'a normalizing society is the historical outcome of a technology of power centred on life' (144). Yet, if the essential purpose of biopolitics is increasing the health of populations, this proliferation of vitality comes at the price of excluding those deemed 'abnormal'. In this respect, Foucault's account of the biopolitical normalisation of life explains how disability becomes 'the master trope of human disqualification in modernity' (Snyder and Mitchell 2006: 125). While Foucault's narrative of the genesis of biopolitics focuses on the emergence of biology and the study of populations, Tobin Siebers has argued that aesthetic judgements concerning the appearance of bodies helped establish and reinforce normative conceptions of human life in modernity. What Siebers calls the 'aesthetics of human disqualification' refers to the representation of disability as 'a marker of otherness that establishes differences between human beings not as acceptable or valuable variations but as dangerous deviations' (2010: 22–4). In the twentieth century, the most glaring example of devaluing disabled bodies coincided with biopolitical catastrophe in 'the Nazi system of disqualification' (29).

It is no coincidence that Nazism enlisted 'the aesthetics of human disqualification' in its drive to craft the eugenic 'Aryan' body of the

German people. 'Eugenics has been of signal importance to oppression', Siebers writes, 'because [it] weds medical science to a disgust with mental and physical variation' (2010: 28–39). Evidence of disgust towards non-standard bodies in Nazi propaganda discloses the way the 'aesthetics of human disqualification' – combined with the biopolitical paradigm of the Third Reich – worked to exclude 'degeneracy' from the collective body of the German nation. Hitler 'embraced health and racial homogeneity as the measures of quality human beings. Disease and disability were his principle disqualifiers' (29). The Nazi regime's commitment to bodily perfection consisted in a lethal programme of racial regeneration which united aesthetic censorship with eugenicist policies in a dual assault on 'dysgenic' form. Nazism thus extended the reach of aesthetic judgement beyond its traditional sphere of authority and used it as the basis for excluding bodies encoded as 'defective' (28–39). Crucially, the interweaving of 'degeneracy' and aesthetics that began with Nordau reached its conclusion in the Third Reich:

> *Degeneration* was principally a medical term before Max Nordau applied it to art. It referred throughout the last half of the nineteenth century to individuals who departed from norms of human health because of genetic difference, sexual habits deemed excessive, or shattered nerves. The Nazis applied these distinctions as standards of aesthetic beauty. Degenerate art deserved its name because it included bodily deformities, bloodshot eyes, feebleness and signs of nervous exhaustion – all disabling conditions supposedly brought about by racial impurity or the stress of modern life. Jews, homosexuals and criminals were automatically assumed to be biologically inferior, and the Nazis found evidence of their assumptions in the physical traits given to people in works of modern art. (Siebers 2010: 31)

The aesthetic devaluation of disability mirrored the idea that the degenerate type was biologically unviable. Nordau anticipated Nazism by envisioning a future purged of bodily and mental 'defects', which meant that those 'outside' the norm, the so-called degenerates, would be consigned to the past as figures of anti-futurity. For Nordau, the tainted hereditary line 'does not continually subsist and propagate itself, but, fortunately, is soon rendered sterile, and after a few generations often dies out before it reaches the lowest grade of organic degradation' ([1892] 1993: 16). This grim prognosis pinpoints a connection between organic decomposition and the sterile exhaustion of the 'abnormal' type. For Nordau, then, the 'degradation' of organic form results in a self-annihilating drift towards death and the erasure of biological futurity. In this way degeneration theory brings the regression of the species and the termination of the non-standard body into a fatal alignment sealed by a double logic of self-destruction.

Just as Nordau locates the visible signs of degeneracy in 'deformities', 'stunted growths' and physical 'asymmetry', so the National Socialists represented the 'abnormal' type as a body without 'proper' form ([1892] 1993: 17). In his *Third Person*, Roberto Esposito argues that Nazi biopolitics conceived of degenerate life as 'a counter type, defined by its original deformation or by the absence of form, which reduced it to simple living material' (2012: 57). Like Giorgio Agamben in his influential *Homo Sacer* (1998), Esposito locates the 'thanatopolitical' core of Nazism in the extermination of bare life. What distinguishes Esposito's account of Nazi biopolitics is his claim that the regime substantiated its acts of genocide by reducing the 'degenerate', 'non-Aryan' body to 'dead life or death that lives, a flesh without a body' (Esposito 2008: 134). Here Esposito's crucial distinction between the body and the flesh comes into view. If Nazism conceived of the racial body as a self-enclosed and purified form, it imagined that degenerate 'life inhabited by death is simply flesh, an existence without life' (134). It was National Socialism's fanatical attachment to the organicist idea of the body, along with its quest to translate 'Jew' and 'abnormal' into synonyms for 'life unworthy of life', which resulted in the genocidal violence of the camps and, ultimately, the self-destruction of the Third Reich: 'the life unworthy of life is existence deprived of life – a life reduced to bare [*nuda*] existence' (134). As Esposito puts it, 'Nazism treated the German people as an organic body that needed a radical cure, which consisted in the violent removal of a part that was already considered spiritually dead' (10). Deformation was thus the danger from which the 'Aryan' body had to free itself in order to attain spiritual perfection:

> The supreme spiritual value for a race is to achieve the perfect form of its somatic features, because this shape is nothing other than the expression of the realization of the truth of the idea, of the type, of the soul of the people. (Forti 2006: 15)

As a result, the spiritualisation of Germany's formed body contrasted absolutely with the de-spiritualisation of 'non-Aryan' flesh.

What is crucial for our purposes here is that the obsession with the spiritualisation of bodily shape or form that defines the Nazi politics of life directly correlates with their notorious campaign against 'degenerate art' (Michaud 2004: 12–13). The Nazi preference for classical aesthetic form mirrored a revulsion with the fractured surfaces of avant-garde painting and sculpture (Siebers 2010: 5). Many Nazi ideologues expressed hostility towards modernist form, because they viewed it

> as the wrong kind of representation of the wrong kind of bodies; a racial, eugenic, and biopolitical notion that takes us directly from the expropriation and destruction of paintings and sculptures deemed degenerate to the elimination of life deemed unfit to live. (Levi 2014: 50)

In a declaration on the future of German *Kultur*, Hitler insisted, 'We want only the celebration of the healthy body in art' (Siebers 2010: 29). Within this racialised vision of aesthetics, Jewish or non-Aryan art is in essence defined as a celebration of crime, weakness, and pathology: 'It practices the glorification of all vices and monstrosities', Joseph Gobbels argued, 'rais[ing] to the level of an artistic ideal whatever is nonheroic, ugly, sick, and decomposed' (in Michaud 2004: 152). Michaud claims that the notion of life imitating art underwrites the Nazis' approval of classical aesthetics and their campaign against 'degenerate art': 'just as the ideal of Greek art ought to necessarily to be embodied in [Hitler's] people, so too it was at all costs necessary to prevent degenerate art from engendering monsters' (152). As such, Nazi ideologues established a mimetic relation between art and the body politic of the Third Reich, whereby artistic form actively *produces* rather than merely re-presents the ideal form of the healthy 'Aryan' body.

When Beckett visited Germany in 1936–7, he wrote in his diaries about the restrictions that the Nazi regime imposed on the public exhibition of modernist art. Although the censorship of 'non-Aryan' painting and sculpture limited his access to particular works, he was nevertheless able to view a number of modernist paintings in galleries which did not comply with the official policy (Nixon 2011: 137). More importantly, Beckett directly encountered the Nazis' attempts to strip modernist art of its cultural value during his trip, for, while he left Germany several months before the notorious 'Degenerate Art' exhibition in Munich, he visited the 'Schreckenskammer des Entarten (Chamber of Horrors of Degenerate Art)' in the Moritzburg in Halle in January 1937' (Nixon 2011: 136). These were 'special shows where the respective inventory of modern art, regardless of its style, was presented in order to defame it' (Zuschlag 1997: 212). With this demotion of modernism to the non-status of abjection, the

Nazis placed non-mimetic art beyond the bounds of cultural decency. Those who promoted the rejection of modernism presented the censorship of 'degenerate art' as a reassertion of traditional norms of respectability and decorum after the cultural and social decadence of the Weimar Republic (212). As the name 'Chamber of Horrors' signifies, the propaganda against modernist art worked by arousing negative emotional responses among the German public:

> The most significant aspects of 'Entartete Kunst', if we listen to the Nazis who toured it, were the feelings of revulsion that the artworks were supposed to excite in beholders. These works were revolting, of course, because they used disability to prove the degeneracy of modern existence. (Siebers 2010: 39)

Because 'Dada and Expressionism deform the bodies rendered by them, seeming to portray disabled people', the Nazis presented these avant-garde movements as monstrous aberrations intent on overthrowing the norms of the purified Reich (Siebers 2010: 35).

Mark Nixon's research on the 'German Diaries' has revealed that Beckett approved of the Expressionist works he viewed during his melancholic artistic pilgrimage in Nazi Germany (2011: 140). His interest was 'not limited to paintings, but extended to the plastic work of Ernst Barlach, whom he appears to have particularly admired' (141). By the mid-1930s, when Beckett was searching for modernist artworks in defiance of the censors, Barlach was one of the many artists under attack from the National Socialists. In the Nazi intellectual Alfred Rosenberg's view, Barlach 'masters his material like a virtuoso [. . .]. But what he designs in the way of human beings, that is alien, entirely alien: [. . .] small, half-idiotically gazing mixed variations of indefinable human types' (in Müller 2014: 181). This reading encodes Barlach's figures as subhuman degenerates, since they violate the Nazi imperative to give a conclusive (i.e. 'Aryan') shape to the human species, while their lack of resemblance to the Nazi-approved type gives rise to anxieties about the dysgenic effects of racial mixing. What is most striking about Rosenberg's negative appraisal of Barlach's sculpture is his palpable sense of disgust in the face of the artist's human figures. Unlike many of the Expressionist artworks which repelled Nazi ideologues, Barlach's figures are not explicitly grotesque or obscene. As Andrew Mitchell explains, 'The degeneracy of Barlach's sculpture lies in the formlessness that literally informs his work. The well-defined faces and hands of these sculptures emerge from the incomprehensible and unexplored masses at their heart' (2010: 92). As the Nazis strived to genetically sculpt 'Aryan' bodies with chiselled outlines, so they rejected sculptures which expose the unshaped materiality of embodied life:

> The National Socialist objection to the earthen nature of Barlach's work is an objection to its unformed massiveness. The earth stands for material that has yet to be taken up and spiritualised. This spiritualisation is an assumption of meaning by the unformed and the meaningless. Making is marking – forming – and the bestowal of meaning is life itself. The healthy life is one that grows ever more definite and meaningful in a meaningful world, growing into the full realisation of its purpose. (Mitchell 2010: 92)

For Mitchell, Barlach's 'work is an act of resistance against the National Socialist drive to form – not, however, by simply asserting the opposite and championing a vague formlessness, but by revealing the limits of form as a contour of reciprocity with the raw matter that lies beyond it' (35). In this way, his artistic negotiation between formed and unformed defies the revulsion against shapelessness which underpins Nazi biopolitics (34).

Like Barlach's plastic art, Beckett's fiction exposes the human form to the 'raw matter' that exists both within and beyond the limits of the body. But what distinguishes Beckett's negotiation between form and formlessness is his inclusion of the abject materiality of corporeal existence in his fiction. The presence of decomposing flesh and bodily effluvia in his work resists the Nazi imperative to exclude disgust-inducing matter from the sphere of cultural production. The 'unformed' – matter without an assigned meaning or purpose, in Mitchell's terms – resists the Nazis' homicidal will-to-form by refusing to answer their call to spiritualise and fix the body. As Purcell suggests, it is also possible to read Beckett's post-war work as 'degenerate art' because he creates literary form by misshaping and distorting it (2015: 39). Degenerate form is always an undoing of form. It represents a kind of negative morphology, whereby formation and deformation are not so much two distinct processes as they are a singular activity of aesthetic de-composition. This aspect of Beckett's aesthetic practice aligns his work with one of the prevailing tendencies of European modernism. As Maren Linett puts it, 'The notion of deforming the contours of what has come before serves as another way to express modernist efforts to "make it new"' (2017: 146).

Yet if the paradox of literary texts which generate form through its degeneration is that the new emerges amidst the breakdown and decay of the old, the modernist affirmation of aesthetic deformity also encodes paradoxical attitudes towards the disabled body. 'Casting nonnormative embodiment as a degraded state', Linett writes, 'many twentieth century artworks nevertheless suggest that this degradation can be transcended through the superiority of modernist art' (200). By contrast, Beckett strives to overturn the idea of art's transcendence of the physical body by making 'degraded' and unformed materiality the primary substance of his post-war fiction. It is this insistence on the base matter of the body which separates Beckett from those modernist artists whose work implies that 'representations of deformity and disability [...] are only acceptable to the degree that they have been transformed into and transcended by art' (Linett 2017: 200). Contrariwise, bodily deformity in Beckett's fiction reminds us of matter's resistance to transcendent ideas of form, shattering the modernist ambition to transmute disability into the 'superior' realm of the aesthetic.

Beckett's refusal of aesthetic sublimation exposes the unadorned materiality of the body. In his 1984 lectures *The Courage of Truth*, Michel Foucault includes Beckett in a tradition of modern painters and writers whose work 'establish[ed] a relation to reality which is no longer one of ornamentation, or imitation, but one of laying bare, exposure, stripping, excavation, and violent reduction of existence to its basics' (2011: 188). According to Foucault,

> there is an anti-Platonism of modern art which was the great scandal of Manet and which, I think, without characterising all art possible today, has been the profound tendency which is found from Manet to Francis Bacon, from Baudelaire to Samuel Beckett or Burroughs. Anti-Platonism: art as the site of the irruption of the basic, stripping existence bare. (Foucault 2011: 188)

Foucault's description of anti-Platonic modern art, I want to suggest, sheds light on Beckett's aesthetic of deformity in his post-war trilogy of novels. For Benjamin Noys, Foucault's account of modern art provides a more compelling model for art's resistance to biopower than the vitalist affirmations of life's radical excess that characterise much of contemporary theory (2015: 170). Noys argues that Foucault's remarks gesture towards 'a counter-form of art developed around the exposure of life', which would involve not only 'a stripping bare of existence, but also a stripping bare of language or visual expression. What Barthes called a 'writing degree zero' [...] converges with life degree zero, or "bare life", to use Agamben's formulation' (170). This conflation of 'bare life' with stripped-down literary form opens up a number of questions. What would an aesthetics of bare life look like? How might we begin to work through the paradox of an aesthetic form that is capable of expressing formless life?

Before answering these questions, it is worth noting that the modernist artists and writers whom Foucault refers to – Manet, Bacon, Baudelaire, Burroughs and, of course, Beckett himself – all made flesh a central concern of their work. These modernist pioneers who helped dismantle 'social norms, values, and aesthetics canons' were also engaged in deforming the normative image of the human body, which aligns Foucault's 'counter-tradition' of art with the modernist aesthetics of disability (2011: 188). So, before Agamben developed his philosophy of 'bare life' and his magisterial account of modern biopolitics, Foucault had already adumbrated an aesthetics of bare flesh – electing Beckett as one its patron saints. The acts of stripping away and laying bare are crucial to Beckett's portrayals of counter-normative embodiment. Beckett's bodies lose their functionality, lose their form, and thereby lose their taxonomic classifications. Nevertheless, the various acts of subtraction that Beckett performs on his fictional creatures leave a surplus of unclassifiable life: a formless remainder which is, so to speak, unnameable.

Over the years, critics have given different labels to the carnal remainder which is the Beckettian body – the monstrous, the posthuman, the creature (Gibson 1996; Effinger 2011; Anderton 2016). My contention is that the reduction of bodies to the 'formlessness' of 'bare life' in Beckett's writing requires us to rethink the idea of form in *The Unnamable* in terms of an aesthetic practice of decomposition, an ongoing effort to 'lay bare' excluded life through an art of misshaping. If, as Noys has put it, Foucault's counter-art of exposed life 'does not so much rest on the supposed plenitude of life overflowing the text, but a baring or voiding of life as value' (2015: 50), then Beckett's stripping away of bodily form can be seen as an accommodation of denuded life in the wake of World War II. In light of these remarks, I want to suggest that articulating a Beckettian resistance to biopolitics would not consist in an affirmation of life liberated from the norm; on the contrary, it would involve tracing how his aesthetic of deformity exposes readers to life stripped of value.

No aspect of *The Unnamable* signifies the stripping away of art's transcendent aspirations more than the anarchic, uncontainable flesh of Beckett's creatures. Just as these distorted beings do not fit the mould of the 'human type', so their unruly flesh continually exceeds the perimeters of the sealed-off body. *The Unnamable* draws our terrified attention to the malleability of the flesh, rearranging body parts in ways which diverge extravagantly from the image of the human as an enclosed, unified being. Beckett's stripping apart of the 'carnal envelope' explodes the anthropomorphic image of the completed human form, as does the severing of the unnamable's nose, eyes, mouth, genitals, arms, hair, and legs from the trunk of its body (Beckett 2010b: 43; hereafter U). We thus encounter flesh beyond the boundaries of the skin, and a series of body parts that do not on any occasion add up to an organic body. Rotting flesh and other putrescent substances offer a further source of unshaped matter, which infuses the text with 'the stench of decomposition' (U 30). And if the unnamable's tormentors describe it as having 'no human shape' (U 94), this is because they are surrogates for Beckett's own stripping away of fleshy material. It has been argued that the unnamable's loss of human identity and exposure to unthinkable acts of torture closely parallel Agamben's account of the 'bare life' of the 'Muselmann' in the Nazi concentration camps (Garrison 2009: 104). Thus, David Houston Jones claims that in *The Unnamable* 'humanity is no longer distinct from animal life (or "bare life", in Agamben's terms)' (2011: 61). While this reading takes account of the stripping away of life's value in the context of post-Holocaust Europe, Beckett's reduction of the flesh to a stripped-down condition of unformed matter in many ways exceeds the figure of animalisation – hence, for example, the description of Worm as 'being less than a beast' (U 72).

Rather than approaching the subject of 'bare life' in terms of the human/animal distinction, I argue that Esposito's configuration of 'bare life' as 'flesh without a body' illuminates Beckett's assault on human form. *The Unnamable* presents the monstrous body as both a scandalous distortion of the human and an unformed mass of matter. Beckett thus conceives of 'bare life' as stripped-raw lumps of flesh without a conclusive bodily form. While I agree with Alysia Garrison's observation that 'Life throughout the *Three Novels* gets successively more bare', I find the claim that *The Unnamable* puts forward 'an ethical critique of the conditions that gave rise to the Holocaust' less persuasive (2009: 97, 102). Indeed, I would argue that Beckett's stripping away of the flesh implicates his art in violence rather than removing it to a transcendent standpoint of ethical purity. In many ways, National Socialism's broadsides against degenerate art prefigure Beckett's post-war vision of misshapen flesh.

Consider, for example, Adolf Hitler's statement that it 'is not the mission of art . . . to wallow in filth for filth's sake, to paint the human being only in a state of putrefaction, [. . .] or to present deformed idiots as representatives of manly strength' (in Linett 2017:

146). There is a teeming mass of liquefied flesh, putrefaction and monstrous embodiment running throughout Beckett's novel. He thus aggressively defies the Nazi conception that aesthetic form is what gives value to life. Instead, he implicates the process of aesthetic formation in the stripping away of life's value. Beckett seeks to fashion a text in which form emerges from deformity, where the narrator is a misshapen 'artist' who in turn misshapes other creatures. It is therefore possible to view the unnamable not just as a degenerate body but also as a degenerate *artist*. Garrison argues that 'Beckett may have made something like the degenerate body the protagonist of his *Three Novels*, but he performs an ethical reversal on Nordau's theory in *The Unnamable*' (2009: 102). By contrast, I argue that Beckett implicates his aesthetic practice in the devaluation of degenerate life. As the unnamable is a deformed creature, so its 'artistic' creations cannot be assimilated within the contours of the 'normal' body: 'before executing [Mahood's] portrait, full length on his surviving leg, let me note that my next vice-exister will be a billy in the bowl, that's final, with his bowl on his head and his arse in the dust' (U 26).

This shift from a portrait of Mahood's one-legged body to an allusion to a legless Dublin beggar suggests a tendency towards an ever-greater fragmentation of the flesh. The process of de-creation continues with the appearance of Worm, who provides the novel's most radical example of a being defined by its lack of form, since this enigmatic being is described as 'shapeless heap, without a face' (U 71), and even as a 'tiny blur' (U 73). Beckett's characters appear as monstrous beings, as figures of excess and deficiency, losing limbs or sprouting fleshy protuberances: 'A head has grown out of his ear, the better to enrage him, that must be it. The head is there, glued to the ear, and in it nothing but rage, that's all that matters, for the time being' (U 70–1). The unnamable has meanwhile 'lost all [its] members' (U 49) and describes itself as 'human to be sure, but not exaggeratedly' (U 27). Paradoxically, the ever-shifting flesh on display in the novel provides a sense of continuity and discontinuity: 'the one-armed one-legged wayfarer of a moment ago and the wedge-headed trunk in which I am now marooned are simply two phases of the same carnal envelope' (U 43). Just as the misshapen narrator repeatedly changes form and yet remains the same, so the narrative shifts and digresses without losing its relentless momentum, which sets up the deformed body as an analogy for the consistent inconsistency of the narrative.

The more distorted and indistinct the flesh becomes, the more it resists conceptualisation and asserts its bare materiality. Even so,

Beckett confounds this drive towards shapelessness by repeatedly invoking the notion of artistic formation. The tension between the formed and the formless expresses itself in the image of fashioning a human-shaped figure from base matter – 'I'm like dust, they want to make a man from dust' (U 62) – which recalls the Jewish myth of the Golem, and, indeed, throughout the text the relation between material and textual deformity expresses itself as a degenerative process of, in Michaud's terms, 'engendering monsters' (2004: 152). Throughout the novel, these inconclusive lumps of flesh and matter never finally resolve themselves into living forms. Nor do they take shape according to the anthropomorphic blueprint of classical aesthetics. The unnamable envisions the possibility that its tormentors will 'leave [it] lying in a heap, in such a heap that none would ever be found again to try and fashion it' (U 62). It imagines that shapelessness may bring an end to the interminable refashioning of its material being. It is as if amorphous matter both invites and interrupts the will-to-form, thereby invoking the limits of the artist's ability to integrate and contain materiality within a meaningful order. In this way, artistic agency loses its connotations of mastery and appears instead in the guise of incapacity, impairment or non-productivity, and the artist is thus recast in the role of, in Beckett's words, 'a non can-er' (in Shenker 1979: 148).

As Helen Deutsch points out, the second definition of 'deformity' in *The Oxford English Dictionary* is 'misshapen', which gestures towards the idea of 'a negative agency, a body created and abandoned by its author' (2015: 52–3). While Deutsch invokes the trope of *Deus absconditus* to parse the idea of misshaping, her description of a 'negative agency' also resonates with Nazi sermons against 'degenerate' artists. 'Negative agency' is precisely what is at stake in the unnamable's encounters with its 'vice-existers': as artists who produce failed and abandoned forms, they 'don't know what to do with' this unshaped matter in order to animate it with life and meaning (U 62). Moreover, the unnamable's admission that it 'has no technique' suggests artistic incompetence (U 64) – like the incompetence which the Nazis blamed for the presence of deformity in modernist art – though it in fact refers to the narrator's physical and mental impairments, including a complete privation of movement and understanding. If this linkage of disability with a lack of artistic mastery recalls the propaganda against degenerate art, it is also in tune with Beckett's development of an art of failure and impotence after World War II.

As Nixon observes, Beckett's continued to associate aesthetic deformity with the Nazi campaign against degenerate art in the post-war period (2011: 136). In his 1945 essay 'La peinture de van Velde ou le monde et le pantalon', he gives an ironic assessment of abstract painting which echoes the National Socialist rhetoric of degeneracy: 'Ne vous approchez pas de l'art abstrait. C'est fabriqué pas une bande d'escrocs et d'incapables. Ils ne sauraient faire autre chose. Ils ne savent pas dessiner [Do not approach abstract art. It is produced by a gang of criminals and incapables. They would not know how to do anything else. They do not know how to draw]' (in Nixon 2011: 136). It is worth keeping in mind that Beckett's championing of failure and impotence in his post-war work closely parallels these ventriloquised statements. As Purcell has intimated, it is possible to read his deformation of the novel form in his post-war fiction as, in part, a response to the attacks on degenerate art he witnessed in Germany in the mid-1930s (2015: 39). It is certainly difficult not to hear a sardonic avowal of artistic intent in Beckett's statement that 'peinture à deformation est la refuge de tous les rates [painting which distorts is the refuge of all failures]' (in Nixon 2011: 136). Deformation, for the Nazis, was a visible sign of aesthetic failure; for Beckett, in contrast, deformity and failure were essential components of an art that refused to find value in achievement and mastery. If the National Socialists conceived of aesthetic distortion as a symptom of artistic failure, Beckett embraced incapacity and 'failed form' as the defining mode of his art (LII 596). As he told Israel Shenker in 1956, 'I'm not the master of my material' (in Shenker 1979: 148). Contrasting his own work with that of Franz Kafka, Beckett went on: 'The Kafka hero has a coherence of purpose. He's lost but he's not spiritually precarious, he's not falling to bits. My people seem to be falling to bits' (148). Bodily disintegration is, in Beckett's terms, an analogy for his art of non-achievement, an art which derives its form, or better, anti-form, from an 'exploit[ation]' of 'impotence' and 'ignorance' (148). If Nazi violence constitutes one of the definitive contexts for his arrival at an aesthetic of deformity and stripped-bare flesh, his rejection of the 'aesthetic axiom that expression is achievement' may itself be an act of political resistance (148). In *Mein Kampf* (1925), Hitler defines a vision of *Kultur* as 'the realized form in which a race preserved itself' (in Michaud 2004: 76). In 1941, Beckett owned a 'heavily underlined' copy of *Mein Kampf* (Bair 1991: 314), which verifies his close scrutiny of Hitler's propaganda. It is thus conceivable that Beckett's insistence on lowness, debasement, deformity and unachieved form emerged as an assault on the Nazi politics of art.

Let us return to Foucault's remarks about the anti-Platonism of modern art, from Manet and Baudelaire to Beckett, Bacon and

Burroughs. For Foucault, this lineage of nineteenth- and twentieth-century art 'established a polemical relationship of reduction, refusal, and aggression to culture, social norms, values, and aesthetic canons' (2011: 188). It therefore amounts to a 'counter-form of art' which eschews ornament and mimesis to perform a 'violent reduction of existence to its basics' (Noys 2015: 170; Foucault 2011: 188). As we have seen, Beckett's work contains striking examples of this process of distorting, dismantling and laying bare. We have also seen that ideas of degeneracy and deformity were central to Beckett's exposure of denuded life. On the canvases and in the texts of 'anti-Platonic' modernism, the form of human body, which has fallen from the transcendent apex it occupied in classical aesthetics, immerses itself in the messy stuff of material being. The body's reduction to unformed flesh, and the loss of its idealised Platonic outline, shatters the normative aesthetics of human form. This is in part what Foucault finds so powerful about the stripped-bare flesh of European modernism, since it consists in nothing less than a violent refusal of the terms of beauty, respectability, decorum and cultural value.

But it is also possible to take Foucault's remarks about Beckett's 'anti-Platonism' in a biopolitical direction. I have argued that Beckett's deformed modernism exemplifies what Noys calls 'a counter-form of art developed around the exposure of life' (2015: 170). The de-creation of aesthetic and bodily form in *The Unnamable* offers an example of an art of resistance that emerged in opposition to the normalisation of life. But I have also suggested that Beckett was engaged in presenting the body as fleshy material stripped of value. This linking of the devaluation of life to the degeneration of bodily form problematises the notion that Beckett's writing offers an affirmation of life, even life which is 'beyond the normal'. Yet what would happen if, in conclusion, we were to read the 'exposure of life' in Beckett's fiction alongside another one of Foucault's modernist 'anti-Platonists' – Francis Bacon? The striking points of resemblance between Beckett's and Bacon's work when it comes to their disfiguring of the flesh have not gone unnoticed. According to Peter Fifield, in Bacon's and Beckett's work 'there is an emphasis not on the fixed form of the whole as constituted by its individual parts – limbs, hands, feet, and so on – but on its underlying fleshiness; the essential meat of the matter' (2009: 59). 'For both Bacon and Beckett', Fifield tells us, 'the medical exception often provides the physiological exemplar; the distortion stresses the everyday condition of being clothed in tissue' (60–1). I would add that the deformed appearance of the flesh in their work emerged as an indirect (i.e. non-representational) response to the devaluation of life exposed to biopolitical violence. For one thing, Beckett's relentless dismantling of the organicist idea of the body in *The Unnamable* closely parallels Esposito's reading of the politics of flesh in Bacon's painting. From Esposito's standpoint, 'the flight of flesh from the body, both barely sustained and strained to the point of spasms by the structure of the bones, constitutes the centre itself of the paintings of Francis Bacon' (2008: 168). Bacon's paintings of deformed flesh are, according to Esposito, the closest thing we possess to an accurate portrait of 'the biopolitical practice of the animalization of man carried out to its lethal conclusion' (168). Yet Bacon's exposure of flesh stripped of value points towards another way of thinking life which would leave behind the idea of the self-enclosed body, whether individual or collective:

> Flesh is the body that doesn't coincide with itself (as Nazism wanted [. . .]), that isn't unified beforehand in an organic form, and that is not led by a head [. . .] No. Flesh is constitutively plural, multiple, and deformed. It is also from this point of view that one can begin to imagine an affirmative biopolitics. (Esposito in Campbell and Esposito 2006: 52)

It may be that the exposure of deformed flesh in Beckett's fiction likewise points us beyond the organicist idea of the body towards a 'life in common'.

Chapter 4

Beckett, Evangelicalism and the Biopolitics of Famine

Seán Kennedy

In *Samuel Beckett and the Politics of Aftermath* (2018), James McNaughton has produced one of the finest monographs on Beckett to date. Just one year after Emilie Morin restored Beckett to his political milieu, in *Beckett's Political Imagination* (2017), McNaughton reads the majors work in light of that milieu (2018: 3). Taken together, these two represent a coming-of-age for Beckett studies. They put Beckett's engagement with politics at the heart of his achievements, helping to explain, along the way, why so many *engagé* artists and philosophers have considered him an exemplary figure. Morin's book recovers so many neglected contexts for Beckett's work, and is so rich in suggestive detail, that it will remain indispensable for years, while McNaughton's take on Beckett's 'radical political intelligence' is an ethical experience in itself (2018: 24). Here, responding to McNaughton's book specifically, I want to offer a different reading of the relevance of the Irish famine to the composition of *Watt* and *Endgame*.

Ireland displaced?

McNaughton's book is notable for its engagement with the logic of Irish exceptionalism. Much of the ethical force of his argument inheres in the corrective it offers to anyone who thinks Ireland a sufficient context for the comprehension of Beckett's post-war work. Here he joins Morin (2009), but also Andrew Gibson (2010a, 2015), whose work on Vichy France did so much to clarify the limitations of the so-called Irish Beckett approach. In two chapters of his book, those on *Watt* and *Endgame*, McNaughton addresses the issue of famine and similarly extends the field to Beckett's 'direct encounter with contemporary politics' (2018: 3). *Endgame* is read as an enactment – an interrogation of the rhetoric – of food politics in Stalin and Hitler's Europe of the 1930s and 1940s (11), displacing previous readings that looked to Ireland for the famine context of the play (Pearson 2001). Ireland does appear in McNaughton's account: it's relevance is 'clear' (2018: 163). However, the force of his reading inheres in its analysis of rhetorical models that, he suggests, Beckett derived from 'recent political ideologies' (131).

This is also true in the case of Beckett's other great famine text, *Watt* (1953), which, McNaughton suggests, has its setting in 'neutral Ireland' but is actually concerned with the problem of Nazi propaganda (2018: 64). As 'an unlikely place to examine fascism', Ireland is chosen in critique of its wartime policy of neutrality: the idea that 'its relationship to the horrors unfolding in Europe [was] one of assumed exception' (68). If *Watt* is a war book, McNaughton suggests, it is in the sense that most of its characters spend much of their time seeming to deny the fact. From this 'strangely benign Irish perspective' (67), the machinations of Nazi propaganda fall into stark relief. Here again, Ireland appears, but only as background. McNaughton does admit the Irish famine as 'important' to an understanding of the book, and says outright that Ireland 'is not simply a blank space to analyse problems abroad' (68). However, he seems less convinced – and as a result less convincing – of this. This may be because he feels Irish materials have already been accounted for, but there is also a sense that he finds them less immediately relevant. Even as it is mentioned, the overall effect, across two chapters, is to displace Ireland in favour of contemporary considerations. McNaughton says we 'need not feel like we have to choose' between Ireland and Europe (68), but his own readings tend to do so: 'Setting *Watt* in Ireland provides a convenient space to dislocate and evaporate obvious and recent political history' (63); 'the genocide that *Endgame* primarily writes from [. . .] draws from 1930s and 1940s food politics' (11). The resulting work is extraordinary in its perspicacity and force. However, so forceful is the corrective offered that Ireland's full significance to the questions McNaughton leaves us with may be obscured.

At the end of his book, McNaughton asks whether Beckett discerned continuities between the policies and legacies of Hitler and Stalin on the one hand, and nineteenth-century colonialism on the other (162–3). One of the aspirations of *Endgame*, he suggests, is to 'confound how we categorize atrocity' (160). Beckett is interested in the 'moral litmus of intention' that is used to discriminate between available methods of 'population management', such as weaponised famine or death camps (162). Foucault would parse this as the distinction between 'taking life' and 'letting it die' (2003: 239–64). For McNaughton, '*Endgame* performs, with dazzling failure, the rhetorical contortions needed to make weaponized famine appear natural' (2018: 161): a rejoinder to Hitler and Stalin both. Ireland and India return at the end of this account, as parties to a question: 'When Clov looks out Hamm's window to report the world outside as "corpsed", is it misleading to read the famine fate of colonial India or semicolonial Ireland as well as that of the steppes?' (161). McNaughton asks, but does not answer the question. Here, I want to argue that Beckett did discern such continuities, and that Ireland was the place where he recovered the personal stakes of what that meant. For McNaughton, one of the principle ways Beckett responds to atrocity is to show how aesthetics, by deigning to be above politics, ends up ratifying particular versions of it. This is the real satisfaction of his take on Beckett's probing of complicity. In a vivid formulation, he sees Beckett's entire literary enterprise 'clasped in the tongs of political complicity [and] forced to explain what it might otherwise ignore' (11). The image is of him torturing his own work to ethical purpose, and it brings us closer than ever before to understanding the form Beckett's post-war aesthetic takes. Beckett's political insights are 'written deeply into the structure' of his writing (14): at the level of 'narrative and symbolic logic' (Valente 2002: 9).

In all of this, and this will be my main contention, Ireland is more than a backdrop, or given instance of a problem. Rather, it is a kind of psychic navel to which Beckett retreated whenever he needed to understand. When Beckett was writing *Watt*, for example, 1940–3, events in Europe were still unfolding – the moment of aftermath had not yet arrived. He did not know what was happening, but he appealed to Ireland in his attempts to understand it. The sheer weight of Irish materials in the manuscripts makes this case. By the time of *Endgame* (1957), Ireland might reasonably be expected to have disappeared from view, since there was so much else to take in; yet Beckett still used it to work through the horrors McNaughton describes. Hence the 'interpretative collision' set up between contemporary food politics and nineteenth-century contexts for famine (McNaughton 2018: 201, 161). In the past, this might have been taken to confirm Beckett's claim that he had no sense of history (in an unpublished letter to Thomas McGreevy, 4 September 1937), or to situate his work 'outside of the possibility of history itself' (Morin 2009: 10). For McNaughton, however, Beckett is asking whether Stalinist and Nazi food politics have 'an analogue, or even an aetiology, in the legacy of nineteenth-century colonialism' (2018: 161).

In one of many compelling insights, McNaughton parses Beckett's donation of manuscripts to the University of Reading as a way of undoing his own 'intent of undoing' of historical materials: 'to show that perhaps we over-privilege erasure as a gesture of universalizing' (20). This seems exactly right. And what the manuscripts of this period reveal, most of all, is that Beckett's method was deliberately anachronistic. What McNaughton says of *Endgame*, is true generally: disparate historical elements are 'jarringly interspersed' producing 'uneasy confusion' (138–9). References to Victorian Ireland occur in contiguity with references to 'the present'. In psychoanalytic terms, rather than displacing such materials, the texts work to *condense* them. Displacement operates by way of substitution, one thing for another: there is a primary object and its substitute(s). In condensation, issues of primacy are deliberately obscured: events that ought to exist in historical sequence are presented simultaneously (Laplanche 2011: 136). This provides a different way, to borrow McNaughton's own phrase, of 'reanimating [the] critical dialectic' between the disparate materials that make these works difficult to situate (2018: 20): 'Kov' is not *either* a homophone of Cobh *or* a reference to a Ukrainian village: it is both. If this makes the setting 'hard-to-pin-down' (163), it also shows Beckett thinking through many things at once. Where historical materialism sees confusion, psychoanalysis sees the condensed eloquence of the symptom. It is a question of emphasis but finally, too, of significance. Where McNaughton contends that we 'need not' choose between Irish and European contexts, the logic of condensation intimates that we cannot: they are inseparable for the purposes of analysis. In the unconscious, where there is no sense of time, there is no sense of anachronism. The result is the profound disorientation of historical/narrative forms of the kind McNaughton discerns in Beckett's writing, and the bewilderment of all this more accurately reflects the manuscripts, as well as Beckett's state of mind as he was writing them.

Evangelical biopolitics

Much of the power of McNaughton's book, I have said, stems from its critique of Irish exceptionalism. Yet, we should not allow the justness of this emphasis to obscure certain (immediately relevant) aspects of Irish *exceptionality*. One is the peculiar nature of Ireland's colonial position vis-à-vis nineteenth-century British colonialism. McNaughton, after Derek Attridge and Marjorie Howes, describes it as 'semicolonial' (2018: 161). A better term, if only because it does not suggest that colonialism comes in fractions, is 'metrocolonial'. Before 1800, as Joseph Valente has it, settlers in Ireland were unusual among colonialists in considering themselves subjects of their adopted homeland – as Irish – but instead of pushing on to independence, as in America or Australia, they sought to reintegrate with Great Britain under the Act of Union. From this point on, Ireland assumed the 'unique and contradictory position' of a domestic colony (Valente 2002: 3). Ireland was, at one and the same time, 'a prized if troublesome colonial possession and a despised but active constituent of the greatest metropole on earth' (3). From then until 1922, the Irish found themselves 'at once agents and objects, participant-victims as it were, of Britain's far-flung imperial mission' (3).

Another related way in which the Irish were exceptional was their status in the discourses of race that did so much to legitimate that mission. Constructed as simian, for the purposes of comparison to colonial others from Africa and elsewhere, the Irish were, nevertheless, white, confounding the distinction – the epidermal schema – underpinning racialised discourse. Famously in 1860, Charles Kingsley lamented the sight of Ireland's 'human chimpanzees' because 'to see white chimpanzees [was] dreadful', while Thomas Carlyle described the Irish as 'white negroes' (in Lloyd 2019: 82). As such, they were a destabilising anomaly in racial discourse. They aroused, with singular intensity, the ambivalence at the heart of the colonial project (Bhabha 2004: 121–31), troubling the discourse of 'assimilation' it enjoined (Lloyd 2019: 83). If the Act of Union suggested the Irish could (and should) be absorbed into the political nation of Great Britain, subsequent government policy, most notoriously during the famine, intimated that they should not. By the mid-nineteenth century, and the outbreak of potato blight, colonialism had been the defining context of Irish existence for over three centuries and, for much of that time, the Irish *were* an exceptional case: exceptionally close, in geographical and racial terms, and exceptionally troublesome. But also, as full members of the Union, exceptionally difficult to wash one's hands of. All of which complicates questions of complicity (and hence neutrality) in Ireland's relation to British colonialism. The idea that Beckett was simply 'against' Irish neutrality, or saw it as manifestly indefensible at the time, is belied by the complex manner in which references to imperialism, colonialism and republicanism coexist in his writings. He has the French Malone think of Terence McSwiney's death on hunger strike in Brixton prison in 1920, for example (1979: 275). As white (but not-quite) participant-victims of British colonialism, the Irish were a special case (which is not to say that they were (or are) special). In this context, further elaboration of the links between British colonialism, German fascism and Russian socialism becomes possible.

Critical to the development of all three 'isms', as McNaughton intimates, is the emergence of biopolitics. In *Society Must Be Defended* (1976), Foucault traces the emergence, in the mid-eighteenth to nineteenth centuries, of a new mode of governance. Where sovereign power wields the power to kill – to 'take life or let live' (Foucault 2003: 241), and disciplinary power is directed at individual bodies (242), biopower entails the power to 'make live and to let die' at the level of population (241). Under biopolitics, the value of life is, at one and the same time, both absolute ('the right to Life') and subject to an ongoing calculus of disposability. Biopolitics decides the value of life, but also how it is to be distributed among object populations: who gets to live, and where, and why, are the variables of its obscene calculus. Obscene because biopolitics produces, as an ongoing effect of its operation, a residuum of more or less disposable bodies (those to be 'let die'), while channelling resources to the production of other, more 'viable' bodies (those to be 'made live'). Determinations of viability occur at the intersection of gender, race, class and dis/ability, with economics playing a decisive role. Often, by way of racialised discourses of scarcity or 'national health', for example, those to be 'made live' are constructed as under threat from precisely those outcasts biopolitics is in the business of producing, reiterating their disposability. A founding contradiction of the biopolitical State, then, is that one must continually earn the right to live even as one's right to Life is deemed absolute. If you fall below the 'poverty line', or are deemed otherwise unviable, you are liable to exclusion: to murder, 'but also [to] every form of indirect murder, the fact of exposing someone to death, increasing the risk of death for some people, or quite simply, political death, expulsion, rejection, and so on' (256). Predicated on a purportedly rational series of calculations about supply and demand, biopolitics, like political economy itself, always evokes a supplementary morality: a theory of what a good life (or 'healthy nation') should look like. In the nineteenth century, this supplement was usually provided by religion. Nietzsche's *Genealogy of Morals* highlighted the founding links between debt and morality ([1886] 2003: 39). Biopolitics exploits those links to rationalise poverty as being, ironically enough, earned.

In this same period, biopolitics became relevant to the so-called Irish question. From early modern times, Ireland had been a steady focus of British colonial policy. As early as 1596, in *A View of the Present State of Ireland*, Edmund Spenser advocated man-made famine as a means to Irish subjugation, predating Stalinism by 350 years. In Book V of *The Faerie Queene*, widely recognised to reference Ireland, he supplemented those efforts with an 'exemplary glorification of violence when employed in a worthy cause' (Canny 1983: 18). Indeed, Spenser – as poet, humanist and would-be genocidalist – embodies with singular clarity the issue McNaughton is most interested in: 'literature's complicity in naturalizing and justifying historical suffering' (2018: 23). By 1845, however, Ireland was not only a colony, but also the homeland. It was a laboratory in which certain kinds of domestic policy, including early experiments in biopolitics, could be tested (Bigelow 2003). But not, any more, the kind of place where people could be summarily killed. And it was at this time that the finer distinctions of the biopolitical calculus – 'to make (Ireland) live, we must let (the Irish) die' – came to shape British policy. Here, Protestant evangelicalism offered the necessary supplement: rationalising the unequal distribution of viability as a function of personal, religious and racial character traits ('lazy Irish Catholic'), rather than, say, the logic of capital, or settler colonialism, or inheritance law. Spenser was genocidal, and openly so. In a sombre assessment of British policy makers during the famine, Peter Gray underlines that 'their intention was not genocidal' (1999: 331). Rather, in ways that anticipate fascism particularly, it was regenerative: 'God and nature had combined to force Ireland from diseased backwardness into healthy and progressive modernity' (331).

This logic of regeneration was evangelical in origin, transposing ideas of personal redemption – rebirth, renewal, death and/as resurrection – into the biopolitical domain. A main Irish grievance in the wake of the famine was that political economy played the decisive role. 'Ireland died of political economy', John Mitchell famously suggested (Ó Gráda 1999: 6). But he might have said evangelicalism. That successive governments failed in their first order of duty – the prevention of mass death by starvation – is 'unquestionable', and was the verdict of many at the time, including Prime Minister Russell (Gray 1999: 333). Yet, Russell had repeatedly tried to do more, and better, for the Irish, but he was finally unable to defeat the prevalent assumption that the event was God's will. For these 'moralists', the famine was a salutary event: a necessary catastrophe brought about by God to instigate a much-needed revolution in Irish character and society (Gray 1999: 104, 286). In January of 1847, at the famine's height, *The Economist* observed: 'To convert a period of distress, arising from natural causes, into one of unusual comfort or ease, by the interference of government money, or of private charity, is to paralyze the efforts of the people themselves' (Ó Gráda 1999: 77). As a founding assumption of most efforts at relief during five years of famine, this was devastating.

In this account, the right thing to do . . . was nothing. Failing that, more or less ambivalent attempts at relief, 'too little, too slow, too conditional', were the best to be hoped for (Ó Gráda 1999: 49). Relief was tantamount to interference. By 1847, with death at catastrophic levels, Charles Wood (Chancellor of the Exchequer), Earl Grey (Colonial Secretary) and Charles Trevelyan (Assistant Secretary to HM Treasury), all held versions of the same view:

> Unless we are much deceived, posterity will trace up to that famine the commencement of a salutary revolution in the habits of a nation long singularly unfortunate, and will acknowledge that on this, as on many other occasions, Supreme Wisdom has educed good out of transient evil. (Trevelyan 1848: 1)

Irish death was merely a prelude to Irish 'regeneration' (Trevelyan, in Gray 1999: 286). In this way, the evangelical tendency contributed much to the death toll. Not that 'moralism' was the only policy produced or debated at the time – all sorts of things were considered and implemented along the way – but alternative policies could not finally displace economic orthodoxy couched in the language of providentialism. Adam Smith's famous 'hidden hand', it turned out, was the hand of God. The natural laws of the market, as expressed in the laws of political economy, were God's laws, no less than an expression of His Will (and discernible in the vagaries of His Providence). In this, the evangelicals claimed not only to have understood God's works, but also to have anticipated many of His best ideas (a notable feature of Providence was how often it merely served to confirm existing prejudices). In effect, *laissez-faire* economics combined with ethnic racism and evangelicalism to produce a narrative of benevolent neglect (an easy thing to provide in the circumstances). The Irish had neglected themselves, and their fate, as was remarked at the time, was extermination. But 'by neglect' (Gray 1999: 337).

Here, McNaughton's finely attuned questions of intention and complicity converge on Ireland. 'If I don't kill that rat, he'll die' (Beckett 2009a: 41; hereafter E2). 'With this one line', McNaughton observes, Beckett 'closes the difference between setting out to commit murder as a goal, and doing nothing in the face of impending death'

(2018: 162). In this way, *Endgame* 'captures the twentieth century emerging from the nineteenth, whereby the moral litmus of intention seems to dislodge in the equivalency of outcome' (162). It is a fantastic insight. For purposes of colonial governance, is death justifiable? Does letting people die regenerate that people? Do people *need* to die for that regeneration to occur? If so, how many? Ireland was one of the first places such questions were debated publicly, at the level of population, and of policy, as part of the new biopolitics. Evangelicalism offered the cleansing prospect of a final redemption, while Providence provided a rationale for pre-existing prejudices. Is taking life morally equivalent to letting it die? McNaughton ends with a flourish: instead of catastrophe or resolution, Beckett confronts his audience with the seeming collapse of such distinctions. He fixes Clov to the floor with 'interrogatory rigor', refusing 'any group the easy assurance of moralizing superiority' (McNaughton 2018: 163). It is an electrifying conclusion to the book, and a final riposte to any merely existential reading of the text. If we take further account of Beckett's metrocolonial Irish background, however, a different reading becomes possible: Clov's fixity may be an indicator of Beckett's ethical paralysis. In this reading, Clov is motionless because Beckett himself is paralysed, and wants his audience to be paralysed, by the implications of what they have just seen. At the conclusion of *Endgame*, Beckett is not only refusing to administer relief from complicity, he is implicating himself.

Metrocolonial culpabilities

Under metrocolonialism after 1800, Irish subjugation (with all its implications for the colonial subject) was not apportioned equally, tending to split along pre-existing lines of status and privilege. Members of the Protestant minorities 'mainly profited' in the administration of empire (at home and abroad), while the Catholic majority mainly 'suffered their connection as a bitter subjugation, notwithstanding their participation in many British cultural and political institutions' (Valente 2002: 3–4). The Protestant ascendancy, in all its internal variety, were the routine benefactors of the oppression of a majority of their countrymen, while themselves being governed from the colonial centre (as their 'abandonment' during the famine showed). The Catholic majority were the main objects of that oppression, even as they were also agents of the oppression of each other (and themselves) by dint of collaboration with minority interests (as, for example, Catholic landlords' agents during the famine).

Abroad, the Irish ascendancy were in active complicity with the imperial project, even as they were not directly responsible for shaping imperial policy. They informed it, or tried to, through Parliament. But the chief impetus lay elsewhere, among the English parties at Westminster. Meanwhile, the Irish majority were in structural complicity with that imperial project even as/if they resisted it at 'home'. By dint of participation – the Irish Raj, for example – this could become active complicity at any time. Active participation bred deeper complicity (Valente 2011: 19), but doing nothing was not nothing. In the circumstances, complicity took many forms, and responsibility could be hard to take. As participant-victims, the Irish were neither responsible for the imperial project nor exempt from complicity: they could be non-participant benefactors (of primitive accumulation, for example), or unwitting, even unwilling, contributors (via taxation to primitive accumulation, for example). The term 'semicolonial' loses its grip here, because it suggests concepts like semi-complicity. In *Endgame*, McNaughton notes, if Clov *is* the child of Hamm's narrative (the play does not tell us), he would be 'innocent insofar as he was indoctrinated and in servitude, rather than fully complicit, as his easy acceptance of the duty to exterminate both rat and child imply' (2018: 154). Semi-complicit, fully complicit? It is a difficult distinction to maintain. Rather, the Irish were fully colonised at home and, after 1800, in full structural complicity with colonialism abroad (with further occasion for active complicity at home *and* abroad). This adds layers of complexity to the participant-victim status of the metrocolonial, helping to explain Clov's (and Hamm's) predicament at the end of *Endgame*.

Beckett never forgot his reception in London, a Paddy after all, and his experience there underlined the problem: at home, he was the coloniser who belonged in England, in England, the Paddy who belonged at home. It had been Bram Stoker's fate (Valente 2002: 38). It would be Elizabeth Bowen's too: the so-called Anglo-Irish predicament. Reviled at home and dismissed abroad, theirs was an ongoing crisis-of-identification (Curtis 1970). Beckett's family, on both sides, were of the privileged minority, and he often joked about his low church credentials, commenting he was raised 'almost a Quaker' (Gordon 1998: 9). The qualification is important as, during the famine, the Quakers, Jonathan Pim foremost among them, took time to travel Ireland and produced compassionate policy statements about the situation (Gray 1999: 199). It was not the Quakers, but the evangelicals – the 'dirty low church' Protestants of which Beckett considered himself a less-than-shining example (LI 134) – that drove the more pitiless aspects of relief policy in Ireland. 'Truly this was the Lord's doing', said Fitzherbert Filgate of the Royal Agricultural Society of Ireland, 'and it is marvelous in our eyes' (Gray 1999: 287). Comments like this explain why Beckett felt increasingly obliged to betray Protestant ascendancy, refusing not to ask awkward questions about its provenance (McCormack 1994). He was confronting complicity with past atrocities on home soil.

Here again, reading the symptomatics of betrayal, condensation offers a better model than displacement. Watt's pot is an *Eintopf*, as McNaughton demonstrates so well. But it is also a pot for soup, Knott's soup, and the links between soup, famine relief and evangelicalism in Ireland were notorious. Following the Act of Union, at the precise moment Ireland became metrocolonial, it became an 'article of faith' among evangelicals that if the Irish could be weaned off Catholicism, they could be redeemed for modernity (Whelan 1995: 137). The goal was to overcome Ireland's pre-existing, if newly Constituted, ethnic divisions by dint of religious conversion. The movement was conceived along the lines of a second Reformation. Large-scale plans predated the famine by a number of decades, and included the formation of 'colonies'. The west of Ireland was preferred because it was desolate, vulnerable and there were fewer priests (138). Cork was a particular focus, but also Kerry and Mayo. In 1830, the Protestant Colonisation Society opened its doors. Progress was slow, but famine offered the breakthrough they needed. By 1848, as 'starvation, disease and mass eviction [. . .] reduced the west to a charnel house of death' (149), momentum gathered. Catholic priests wrote furious letters that their congregations were driven by starvation to 'take the soup' (149). Souperism became synonymous with cynicism. When the 1851 census showed the Irish population had declined by 1.75 million those who would eliminate Catholicism (the evangelicals) were linked in the popular imagination to the extermination of Catholics through hunger (150). Ironically, soup kitchens were also the most effective means of relief tried by any administration, with three million meals served in one day in 1847. These were soon taken down, however, lest they create a culture of reliance among the destitute (Gray 1999: 266–7). As a child of evangelicalism, Beckett inherited and inhabited this legacy and, in his work, was increasingly driven to respond to it. And all of this is also condensed in Knott's pot.

Evidence of Beckett's working through complicity can be found throughout the manuscripts. Some of it has been mentioned in existing scholarship (Kennedy 2014a). In the case of *Watt*, the landlord called Mr Knott, having been Mr Quin, began life in the drafts as Mr Roe (WMS 1, 5r). This was Beckett's mother's surname. Beckett was himself named after his maternal grandfather, Samuel Robinson Roe, 'widely respected in the farming community [. . .] and much revered on the corn exchange in Dublin' (Knowlson 1996: 2). Confronted with the Nazi invasion of France, and on the run from the Gestapo, Beckett responded by writing a famine novel in which his complicity with colonialism is admitted from the outset. Within the Irish metrocolonial paradigm described above, he begins by deliberately implicating himself in the role of occupier (as descended from Knott, so to speak, rather than Watt; Hamm, rather than Clov). This frank admission is then undone through a series of displacements that cultivate denial: Roe becomes Quin becomes Knott. Here, Beckett is exploring not only the workings of Nazi propaganda, but also the ethical dilemmas of metrocolonialism: where Hamm deflects responsibility, and Watt rationalises away complicity (McNaughton 2018: 61), Beckett confronts both. Commencing his exploration of famine in *Watt*, he *starts* from personal complicity with evangelical landlordism and, by the culmination of *Endgame*, is refusing to exonerate Clov – as participant-victim – from what has been committed. In the metrocolonial predicament, who to blame?

The dialectics of depravity

The English moralists, assessing the Irish landlord and his tenants, had a clear answer: blame both. Once Providence (as God's Englishman) was seen to be at work, the rest of the story wrote itself: Ireland was a place where 'improvident' landlords and their equally improvident tenants had combined to pervert the course of civilised society (Trevelyan 1848: 22). The landlords deserved to die out too (as a class) because they were responsible for the debacle. Parliament's decision, after June 1847, to make relief a function of the Poor Law, thereby passing the buck to the landlords, formalised the growing consensus that they ought to pay for their own mistakes (Gray 1999: 201). Beckett was thinking of William Carleton as he wrote *Watt*, noting his surname above the long sequence given over to the contents of the Quin house (WMS 2, 3v). He even tried on Carleton's signature style ('gintlemin' etc.) for a discourse on one's religious duties if, perchance, a rat should eat a consecrated wafer (WMS 2, 8r). Works like Carleton's *The Squanders of Castle Squander* (1852) are important precedents for Beckett in his treatment of the Irish famine. In the absence of official histories, literature offered a precious (i.e. both valuable and fragile-seeming) resource.

For Carleton, the problem in Ireland lay with human cynicism rather than Divine inscrutability: Irish landlords had neglected to control subdivision on their property, when there was a forty-shilling franchise, because it suited them. The more tenants of forty shillings they had, the more votes they owned. But those tenants needed tenants, too, leading to unsustainable growth among an underclass of the Irish poor: the very ones now deemed 'redundant' (Gray 1999: 279). The moral force of Carleton's case rests in the contention that the landlords have not only 'oppressed' their tenants, but 'corrupted' them too (1852: I, 167). To this process, rather than racial character, he attributes the meaner aspects of the Irish character: the filth, the cunning, the ignorance of order and self-reliance (1852: I, 175). Living in hovels, subsisting on potatoes, they have no reason to aspire beyond mere existence. Carleton's take is founded in the logic of equilibrium that dominated the Victorian mind, shaping everything from political economy to hegemonic constructions of manliness (Gray 1999: 38; Valente 2013: 7). As a kind of outlier in the economic puzzle, 'the infinitesimal system' (1852: II, 11) as Carleton calls it, these squatting classes are, literally, an incalculable risk. He agreed with Thomas Malthus that the potato had contributed to Irish overpopulation (1808: 337), and with the moralists that it was the 'one of the greatest curses ever inflicted upon Ireland' (Carleton 1852: II, 246). In effect, subdivision and the potato had combined to derange the tendency towards equilibrium in the Irish land system. They had decoupled population growth from available resources. The result was a perverting dialectic: the landlords failing in their initial responsibility to the tenants, causing a decline in the economic and moral condition of the Irish poor; this causing the depraved peasants, as they reproduced on a subsistence, to forgo their responsibilities to their betters (1852: I, 10). The inevitable end was bankruptcy, the collapse of the landed classes and a final corruption of the Irish peasantry.

Yet, from the perspective Carleton lays out, with subdivision as the founding error, the obvious solution is consolidation of holdings. Squatters would have to be evicted so that economically viable units of land could be re-created. The problem, then, becomes what to do with the peasantry? Carleton does not deny that consolidation is economically necessary, only that it is unforgivable in the circumstances: equivalent to 'extermination' (1852: II, 82). Having 'connived' in the problem of subdivision, the landlords are morally obliged to their tenants (1852: II, 82). New laws are needed, but the landlords also need to shoulder their weight. Under the Poor Law, the landlords responded, to do so would render them as destitute as their peasants (Gray 1999: 236). The burden of relief was considerable, and not unrelated to the resentment (cynicism?) expressed by Hamm at the end of his tale: 'All those I might have helped' (E2 41). Notoriously, however, William Gregory tabled a successful amendment to the Poor Law which meant that tenants holding less than a quarter-acre had to surrender it to their landlord before qualifying for relief (Gray 1999: 277). Here was an opportunity to clear encumbered holdings. Some felt the operation of the Poor Law left even fair-minded landlords little choice. Others relished the prospect. In Parliament, Lord Clanricarde elicited a 'general shudder' when he spoke of the necessity for systematic ejectments (Gray 1999: 192). The aim was to 'sweep Connacht clean', as Lord Clarendon put it (309). Simply feeding the people had proven 'futile' (309). As predicted, the clause facilitated mass evictions and Gregoryism joined souperism in the annals of famine memory: 'A more complete engine for the slaughter and expatriation of a people was never designed' (Donnelly 1995: 160). Between 1847 and 1850, Carleton informs his readers, '140,101 Irish farms were annihilated by extermination, consolidation, and emigration' (1852: II, 236). In the dialectic of degradation that he places before them, this is not only a gross abdication of responsibility, but a threat to the integrity of the Union. In *Watt*, the state of both Mr Knott and the Lynch family indicates just how far this process of mutual degradation might go.

Among Irish newspapers, the *Freeman's Journal* frankly condemned the Poor Law as allowing 'landlords to evade their responsibilities and *to exterminate the poor*' (Gray 1999: 295, emphasis original). This issue of responsibility, with all its implications for complicity, was keenly contested. From the outset of blight, everyone was blaming someone, most often someone else, and usually Providence. In 1852, George Henry Moore, who had refused to evict any tenants under Gregory, was told outright by his improving cousin: 'you do more to ruin and injure and persecute and exterminate your tenants than any man in Mayo' (in Donnelly 1995: 158). By this light, human compassion was the problem. And such feeble rationalisations only proliferated as the death toll rose. By 1848, Lord Russell had retreated into the language of fatalism: the Irish were being 'disposed of by a higher power' (Gray 1999: 322). Meanwhile, the moralists, who controlled the Treasury, continued to blame the destitute for their own condition. As early as 1846, when blight returned for a second year, *The Times*, an unofficial mouthpiece for this position, claimed the Irish were exploiting famine to abuse English generosity: 'Alas! The Irish peasant has tasted of famine and found it was good' (in Gray 1999: 234). The Irish were so incorrigible that they would rather starve, or beg, than cultivate self-reliance.

Such extraordinary sentiments provide the rationale for Hamm's claim to have put the starving beggar 'before his responsibilities' (E2 49). Had they been to see *Endgame*, *The Times* editors would have known exactly what he meant:

> For our part, we regard the potato blight as a blessing. When the Celts once cease to be potatophagi they must become carnivorous. With the taste for meats will grow the appetite for them; with the appetite, the readiness to earn them. With this will come steadiness, regularity, and perseverance. (In Gray 1999: 227)

Hamm is looking to displace blame, like other Irish landlords of his time. He is not only deflecting Carleton's critique, but also ratifying the moralist consensus regarding the fecklessness of the Irish peasant. If the Irish must insist on planting potatoes in the presence of blight, they must die. Or, as Charles Wood, Chancellor of the Exchequer put it, 'Where the people refuse to work or sow they must starve' (in Gray 1999: 292).

In this light, the relevance of *The Tempest*, as intertext of both *Watt* and *Endgame*, is its acknowledgement of the coloniser's responsibilities *to*, as well as for, the moral condition of the colonised: 'this thing of darkness I acknowledge mine' (Shakespeare [1611] 1988: 130). It is the same dialectic of responsibility outlined in Carleton, and perverted in Beckett. Mr Knott is a sort of on-site absentee landlord. He is present but has failed to control subdivision, as the Lynch family attest. In *Endgame*, however, Hamm is an improving one: 'I enquired about the situation at Kov, beyond the gulf. Not a sinner. Good' (E2 32). Hamm's chronicle borrows widely, too, from rationalisations of the futility of relief. To the extent that nature's laws were political economy's laws, they were ineluctable: 'You're on earth, there's no cure for that!' (E2 33). Together, these two condense the worst excesses of Irish landlordism. Hamm stumbles over excuses, while foisting responsibility onto his victims. He is a bully, a sadist, perhaps even sexually abusive. Knott remains aloof from his tenants, makes occasional gifts of 'loose change and tight clothes' (W 97), while having Watt feed his leftovers to a dog. Meanwhile Clov, suitably depraved by his apprenticeship at Hamm's hands, instinctively moves to enact one final murder: a child. As participant-victim of Hamm's regime he is, at once, both actively responsible and structurally exempt from responsibility for such acts: he cannot be blamed for how he has been indoctrinated, but neither can he be exonerated from what he is about do. In the case of the Irish famine, Beckett reached a similar conclusion in relation to himself: he was neither responsible, nor exempt from responsibility.

This thing of darkness

Beckett's understanding of complicity changed in World War II. In his works to 1939, the Irish famine crops up occasionally, one referent among many. It is only with the outbreak of conflict, and his narrow escape from arrest, that it becomes a pressing subject in its own right. Far from disappearing under the burden of contemporary horrors, it is something Beckett confronts with growing urgency as these play out. It is as if his escape from the Gestapo, the guilt it occasioned, triggered a retroactive reckoning with 'his people's' contribution to Ireland's limit event (Laplanche and Pontalis 1973: 111–14). As metrocolonial occupier, and an evangelical into the bargain, he was implicated in a colonial machine that allowed a million Irish to starve for their own good. Thereafter, a main reason the famine haunts him is the role played by evangelical Protestantism in rationalising the death toll. Pierre Bourdieu calls it 'ontological complicity' (2000: 306). As any German after World War II might attest, complicity is a transgenerational predicament and atonement a transgenerational task. Beckett sees this in a flash. Some among his ancestors would have cheered the prospect of blight, others expressed regret while quietly consolidating their position (Whelan 1995). Guilt was general all over Ireland. And this stark fact grew less easy to ignore as Hitler and Stalin enacted their atrocities.

This was especially so as those atrocities were being couched in practically similar terms. Rhetorically, evangelical Protestantism turned (other people's) death into (their) redemption. In this, it was proto-fascist. 'God and nature had combined to force Ireland from diseased backwardness into healthy and progressive modernity' (Gray 1999: 331). Hitler and 'national destiny' would contrive to do the same for Germany. Here, Beckett is not pitching 'the fantasy of Irish exceptionalism against European atrocity' (McNaughton 2018: 149). Rather, Ireland is the site of a prior convergence of the evangelising rhetoric of national regeneration with the obfuscations of the biopolitical calculus. This is why Ireland matters more than Kipling (157), though Kipling matters too. Ireland is not background, or another instance of a general problem, but intricate to the logic of complicity that Beckett was discovering, by implication, in these works.

Towards the end of his book, McNaughton confronts Clov gazing out on his audience: 'I see ... a multitude ... in transports ... of joy' (E2 20). With this elliptical evocation of the trains to Auschwitz and the Gulag, he argues, Beckett implicates them too (McNaughton 2018: 150). Millions have died, and here we are: in the theatre. This is the precise terrain of McNaughton's distinctive contribution. Beckett, also a survivor, is now a playwright, exercising what McNaughton terms the 'playwright's prerogative': 'the imagine-it-so of aesthetic production' (22). Others, including friends like Alfred Péron, who perished, were not so lucky. And Beckett could not get over it, as McNaughton shows. This is the import of his remarkable account of *The Unnamable* as a narrative voice that would escape guilt but only at the cost of 'destroying all possibility of being born into subjectivity' (108). The sobering conclusion is that there is no outside to survivor guilt, just as there was no outside to complicity as Beckett was coming to understand it. Accordingly, at the end of *Endgame*, Beckett can only hold the various aspects of complicity in suspension (including his own, and that of his audience). He condenses them on stage, but does not, and cannot, move to resolve them. Where Ibsen slams the door, Beckett turns the key. Impasse. Ethically, it is a precise and exacting double bind: 'aporia pure and simple' (Beckett 1979: 267).

Yet aporia are rarely pure and never simple. This one is a variation of the riddle of the heap that Clov and Hamm both puzzle over, and that a metrocolonial, a camp survivor, or a collaborationist, indeed, could not fail to be interested in: when does acquiescence become complicity, for example, or complicity shade into collusion? This, we might say, is the ethical counterpart to the biopolitical calculus. Does complicity by dint of inaction move us closer to exoneration? If so, by how much? If not, does it make a difference? The answer, as Beckett had learned, is that it cannot *not* make a difference. Such are the stakes, and such the terms, that every choice matters, even the ones you don't get to make. Ethics, in this reading, is the always-already-compromised determination to bear responsibility where it cannot be escaped anyway. No more than Beckett, Clov is paralysed by the implications of this: 'I use the words you gave me', he reminds his father (E2 28). But in the circumstances, what to say?

Chapter 5

'He wants to know if it hurts!': Suffering beyond Redemption in *Waiting for Godot*

Hannah Simpson

Physical pain is frequently perceived as an interruption of the 'normal' in modern Western culture. 'The body in pain seeks relief so as to be able to function normally again' (Reyes 2016: 177). Pain-free existence is the 'normal condition that people ought to have restored' (Frank 2013: 77). Yet throughout Samuel Beckett's *Waiting for Godot* (1953) – a play he described to Georges Duthuit as 'a place of suffering' (LII 218) – the characters are in near-constant pain. Vladimir suffers from his prostate infection, Estragon from his too-tight boots and the beatings he endures off-stage, Lucky from his chafed neck and heavy burdens, and Pozzo from his slapstick tumbles in Act II. Arthur Schopenhauer's claim in *On the Suffering of the World* that pain is the typical mode of human existence rings true of Beckett's play: 'order your expectations of life according to the nature of things and no longer regard the calamities, sufferings, torments and miseries of life as something irregular and not to be expected but [. . .] entirely in order' ([1850] 2004: 14). In this Schopenhauerian vein, physical pain is the norm for Beckett's characters.

Alongside its depiction of unrelenting suffering, *Waiting for Godot* emphasises the obstacles to any shared or empathetic experience of pain. Not only do Beckett's characters frequently refuse sympathy to their suffering companions, but the play's staging of the pained body also works to block any potential empathetic response from the spectator. *Waiting for Godot* marks the moment of Beckett's turn to the stage medium after decades of writing primarily in prose. In the theatrical encounter, human suffering is presented via the material facticity of the performer's body, rather than abstractly mediated via the printed text. Faced with the performance of suffering, the spectator is rendered complicit with the spectacle before them, compelled by auditorium etiquette to remain in their seats before the depiction of pain onstage. *Waiting for Godot*, then, both stages and generates unsympathetic responses to pain. This is a very different mode than that suggested by the uncharacteristically sentimental end of Schopenhauer's essay, where recognition of the other as a '*fellow sufferer, compagnon de misère*' should 'instil in us indulgence towards each other', the virtues of 'forbearance, and charity' ([1850] 2004: 15). Rather, in Beckett's play, pain widens an already-gaping gulf between individuals.

In probing the fundamental incomprehensibility of another's pain, and our apparent lack of instinctive compassion, the play evinces a historically contingent pessimism. Beckett wrote *Waiting for Godot* following prolonged confrontation with suffering, both the sectarian violence of Ireland and Northern Ireland (Kennedy 2010; Barry 2005), and the mass slaughter of World Wars I and II (Davies 2020, Gibson 2015): a pattern of recurrent violence that might well prompt an idea of the world as a place of constant suffering. The horrors of World War II in particular were not likely to instil confidence in any redemptive human impulse to compassion, notwithstanding the hasty post-war construction of social and cultural narratives claiming otherwise (Wasson 2010: 15; Rousso 1991: 10). *Waiting for Godot*'s depiction of non-compassionate responses to suffering reflects the historical reality that Beckett witnessed in a France that collaborated with its Nazi occupiers to deport 76,000 of its Jewish citizens (Rousso 1991: 7), an Ireland that refused to lend official support to the war effort, and an England that turned away more than seven times the number of Jewish war refugees that it accepted (London 2000: 12). *Waiting for Godot* does not soften its depiction of our capacity to ignore or recoil from another's suffering. If Raymond Williams found comfort in the fact that 'while men created the [concentration] camps, other men died, at conscious risk, to destroy them' (2006: 82), then Beckett's post-war work suggests an inability or unwillingness to forget that some people did build the concentration camps. We are more likely, a play like *Waiting for Godot* suggests, to perpetuate the suffering of others – even by dint of inaction – than to prevent it.

Examining *Waiting for Godot*'s treatment of pain helps to counter some of the more determinedly optimistic interpretations of the play. The largely redemptive reading that governed its early humanist reception has remained something of a critical norm in Beckett studies; as Paul Sheehan observes, 'the suffering and wretchedness that Beckett's "people" endure, without consolation or rationale, have traditionally been seen as part of a redemptive structure' (2009: 87). Such readings distort the careful delineation of suffering that

Beckett presents and, in doing so, elide its troubling, self-interrogatory charge. Indeed, Beckett himself would recognise and lament what he termed a 'redemptive perversion' in Peter Hall's 1955 Arts Theatre production of the play (LI 573); by contrast, he praised the original Théâtre de Babylone production as 'more like what I wanted, nastier' (LI 611). Even critics who foreground the influence of World War II on Beckett's subsequent writing have insisted on 'redemptive' readings. In his speech at the Swedish Academy granting Beckett the 1969 Nobel Prize for Literature, for example, Karl Ragnar Gierow claimed that the wartime 'degradation of humanity' that Beckett's work traces is the catalyst for 'a love of mankind [. . .] that has to reach the utmost bounds of suffering to discover that compassion has no bounds' (2007: 87). Lois Gordon reads *Waiting for Godot* as 'a product of the war and [Beckett's] response to the complexity of human goodness and evil' which bespeaks 'the obligation to reaffirm one's humanity by helping and protecting strangers and those one loves from gratuitous suffering' (2013: 220). Within this optimistic interpretative framework, physical pain in Beckett's writing has been glossed as a reconciliatory experience that strengthens human affinities, rather than as the isolating, aversive phenomenon that critical pain studies more often delineates.

Such readings ignore both the extent to which the play is saturated with suffering and its foregrounding of our impulse to turn away. Just as the characters onstage recoil from each other's distress, and the spectator so often recoils from the staged performance of pain, so too critics and scholars have recoiled from a clear-eyed consideration of Beckett's depiction of bodily suffering. Theoretical work in pain studies can help us to understand this resistance. Despite the wealth of medical humanities scholarship in analysis of Beckett's work (Barry et al. 2016), pain studies has not yet been fully integrated into Beckett studies. This is a missed opportunity, given the field's pragmatic recognition that pain is isolating and aversive rather than enlightening or 'redemptive': the same uncompromising insight that we have tended to ignore in *Waiting for Godot*.

The struggle to communicate pain

The question of whether physical pain is communicable, or how far one individual's bodily suffering can be recognised by another, has long occupied clinical pain studies, as Roger B. Fillingim observes: 'A well-recognized challenge resulting from the subjective nature of pain is that direct measurement of pain is impossible[;] rather we must rely on individuals' self-report, and to some extent their behaviour, to provide a glimpse into their experience' (2017: S11). Beneath Fillingim's breezy reference to 'self-report' lies a long history of clinical attempts to refine the imperfect process of pain measurement. The McGill Pain Questionnaire developed in 1971, for example, offers an extensive list of scaled adjectives, and asks patients to specify if their pain is 'flickering' or 'quivering', 'pounding' or 'throbbing', 'annoying' or 'troublesome' – and, perhaps most baffling, 'sore' or 'hurting' (Melzack 1975: 279, 281). Contemporary medical practice has largely abandoned the attempt to offer verbal means of expression for pain, with diagnosticians now more commonly providing numerical or pictorial scales as a way of tracking physical discomfort. Even at a clinical level, verbal attempts to communicate pain are riven with difficulties.

Elaine Scarry offers a seminal theory of pain's fundamentally incommunicable nature, its 'unsharability', resulting from its resistance to language (1985: 4). Scarry positions pain as simultaneously indisputable to its sufferer and unverifiable for its witness, something that 'comes unsharably into our midst as at once that which cannot be denied and that which cannot be confirmed' (1985: 4). *Waiting for Godot* stages this unsharability. The tramps' first argument onstage, for example, revolves around the pain each suffers: Estragon in his feet and Vladimir in his prostate. The same exchange is repeated, a few seconds apart, with interlocutors reversed:

ESTRAGON: [*Feebly.*] Help me!
VLADIMIR: It hurts?
ESTRAGON: Hurts! He wants to know if it hurts!
[. . .]
VLADIMIR: I'd like to hear what you'd say if you had what I had.
ESTRAGON: It hurts?
VLADIMIR: Hurts! He wants to know if it hurts! (WG 12)

The exchange emphasises the similarity in their conditions: both are in pain. Simultaneously, however, both men are isolated in their shared-but-distinct suffering. They do not address each other directly, but refer to each other in the third person – 'He wants to know if it hurts!' – denying any potential for intimacy or shared understanding. Each queries, even doubts, the other's experience – 'It hurts?' As Scarry observes, we are free to doubt, even to deny, the pain of others (1985: 4). Where pain is incommunicable, one can only be certain of one's own suffering, and potential for fellow feeling is sorely attenuated as a result. Similarly, the shared 'it' of Vladimir's and Estragon's 'it hurts' may seem to unite the two sufferers in one referent, but only misleadingly so. This 'it' is deictically unstable, shifting referent in each character's enunciation, so that the initial apparent coalescence of referent belies a deeper-rooted gulf in communication. The tramps' exasperation with each other dramatically exemplifies Scarry's theory that the inability to communicate one's own pain or to comprehend another's lessens the individual's capacity for compassionate response.

Where Scarry emphasises pain's resistance to linguistic expression, later pain theorists have turned to the non-linguistic as a means by which pain may be communicated. Pain theorist Javier Moscoso cites the culturally learned non-linguistic expressions of pain, such as weeping, groaning and flinching, as a primary means by which physical pain can be effectively communicated (2012: 6–7). Certainly, *Waiting for Godot* stages the non-linguistic expression of pain: we witness, for example, Vladimir's '*face contorted*' at the stabs of pain from his prostate (WG 13), Estragon '*howling with pain*' (WG 32) and Pozzo's '*cries of pain*' (WG 77). Estragon's '*limping and groaning*' after Lucky kicks him even rouses enough recognition in Vladimir that he can explain to an uncomprehending Pozzo, 'My friend has hurt himself' (WG 82). Perhaps it is unsurprising that the playwright who doubted the expressive capabilities of language (Beckett 1983: 171–2) should privilege the non-verbal expression as more likely to succeed where its verbal counterpart fails.

That said, *Waiting for Godot* does not go so far as to assume that the successful communication of pain, whether verbal or non-verbal, will generate compassion in the observer. When Pozzo lies helpless on the ground during Act II, Estragon and Vladimir remain unaffected by the spectacle, content to calmly ponder the possible benefits that it might offer them:

[POZZO *writhes, groans, beats the ground with his fists.*]
ESTRAGON: We should ask him for the bone first. Then if he refuses we'll leave him there.
VLADIMIR: You mean we have him at our mercy? [. . .] And we should subordinate our good offices to certain conditions. [. . .] That seems intelligent all right. (WG 73)

Vladimir and Estragon remain detached, willing to abandon Pozzo to his distress. Such seeming indifference reflects the social reality of wartime and post-war France, where protracted suffering generated a war-hardened dispassion: 'compassion fatigue' (Kurasawa 2014: 31–2), a kind of 'moral anaesthesia', set in (Marrus and Paxton 1981: 16). Vladimir and Estragon's response to Pozzo enacts a similar indifference, though their preoccupation with scraps of food recalls the terrible conditions of the Nazi occupation (Reggiani 2007: 106). Pozzo's distress offers a rare occasion to alleviate their own suffering. Thus when they do go to his aid, they are not motivated by newfound compassion. Their 'anticipation of some tangible return' is met by Pozzo's promise of financial recompense (WG 74):

> POZZO: Help! I'll pay you!
> ESTRAGON: How much?
> POZZO: One hundred francs!
> ESTRAGON: It's not enough.
> [...]
> POZZO: Two hundred!
> VLADIMIR: We're coming! (WG 75)

Even where another's pain is recognised, nothing in *Waiting for Godot* guarantees a compassionate response from the observer.

Pain's aversive affect

Alongside indifference to another's pain, *Waiting for Godot* also stages the aversive withdrawal from it. Clinical pain studies have emphasised how the sight of physical distress, as a phenomenon against which the body is trained to protect itself, can stimulate a recoil response in the observer: we retreat self-protectively from suffering that threatens to infect us with its negative affect. When 'the distressing, sympathetic feelings associated with opening to the distress of others' are experienced too acutely, the individual can become 'fearfully resistant to compassion' (Gilbert and Mascaro 2017: 401). In Beckett studies, Garin Dowd (2012) has traced how pain isolates the sufferer not by dint of going unrecognised, but rather by being too strongly perceived. The recognition of another's pain frequently causes the observer to turn away: the perception of pain 'produces a countermanding force' (Dowd 2012: 71). Beckett's work, then, demonstrates pain's near-simultaneous engendering of sympathy *and* aversion: sympathy generated by pain is precisely the reason why perceived pain generates aversion. Although Dowd focuses primarily on Beckett's *Texts for Nothing* (1967), we can also trace this tension in *Waiting for Godot*. It is rendered tangible, for example, during Pozzo and Lucky's first slapstick entrance. Their arrival is signalled by the *'noise of LUCKY falling with all his baggage. VLADIMIR and ESTRAGON turn towards him, half wishing half fearing to go to his assistance'* (WG 23).

The threat of pain's contagion undermines the possibility of empathetic response throughout the play. In fact, empathy tends to be punished. In Act I, prompted by Vladimir's outrage over Lucky's 'running sore' (WG 26, 28) and Pozzo's urging 'Comfort him, since you pity him' (WG 32), Estragon approaches the weeping Lucky with a handkerchief. When he attempts to wipe away Lucky's tears, '*LUCKY kicks him violently in the shins. ESTRAGON drops the handkerchief, recoils, staggers about the stage howling with pain*' (WG 32). The moment illustrates the danger of 'feeling pain with' another. Henceforth, Estragon will recoil from the risk of pain's contagion, rebuffing the idea of offering 'pity' throughout the rest of the play. In Act II, he refuses to answer Pozzo's call for help:

ESTRAGON: [*Recoiling.*] Who farted?
VLADIMIR: Pozzo.
POZZO: Here! Here! Pity!
ESTRAGON: It's revolting! (WG 76)

Later, Estragon's dozing off provides motivational grounds for his claiming ignorance as to the nature of Pozzo's plea:

POZZO: Pity! Pity!
ESTRAGON: [*With a start.*] What is it? (WG 77)

Again, Estragon's refusal to acknowledge another being's call for pity is rationalised – he is disoriented on having just woken up – but its ambiguous overtones remain. *Waiting for Godot*'s characters struggle to communicate their pain; when communication *is* achieved, it catalyses aversion rather than sympathy.

Waiting for Godot not only stages the characters' recoil from another's suffering, but also frequently induces the same reaction in its spectators. The specific structure of the theatre medium works to crucial effect here. Drawn into flesh-and-blood confrontation, 'performer and spectator experience each other viscerally, sensually, intuitively, immediately' (Mehta 1994: 184). The results are not always comfortable. Theatrical performance demands a corporeal encounter, bringing the spectator's body into a closer confrontation with the performer's body, posing a heightened threat of pain's contagion. Jean Martin recalls his performance as Lucky in Roger Blin's original 1953 Théâtre de Babylone production:

> I made him stand on one foot, this Lucky, and, as the other foot doesn't rest on the ground, this makes him tremble and that leads to a trembling of the arms, then of the whole body, and to a tremor in his voice, finally to a sort of delirium. (Knowlson and Knowlson 2007: 118)

The trembling that this asymmetrically weighted stance precipitates in Martin's limbs bespeaks his physical struggle in playing Lucky. Steven Connor has noted of trembling that

> its nature is to communicate itself. [. . .] Watching the twitching of an eyelid, the trembling of a pair of hands, it is hard to retain our composure. We seem to feel the action incipiently, as a sensation, a ghostly ripple of sympathy at work in us. (Connor 2008: 209)

Extending Connor's exploration of the emotionally communicative nature of trembling to the material plane, Ulrika Maude observes how a trembling object or body will spread its tremor to whatever it touches; its shaking 'is contagious and spreads over anything that comes into its vicinity' (2009: 96). Trembling breaks down clear boundaries between perceiving subject and trembling object, offering a particularly clear example of corporeal contagion. Martin's painful trembling performance provoked an acute response in his earliest spectators, as his recollection of one particular rehearsal demonstrates:

> four or five days before we were due to open, the costume lady of the theatre was there with her husband [. . .] and as I worked up to my frenzy, because I started calmly, just trembling a little, then at the end finishing in a state of real delirium, at that point the costume lady started to cry out and vomit, saying, 'I just can't stand this'. And Roger Blin said, 'Well, if it has an effect like that, you must keep it!' And we did. (Knowlson and Knowlson 2007: 118)

Martin's expression of physical pain engendered an extreme physical response – and, indeed, a physically painful response – in the unlucky costume designer. Xerxes Mehta has remarked that Beckett's plays tend to 'bring performer and spectator into a unique and unbearable confrontation' (1994: 179); the key word here is 'unbearable'. Pain's contagion stimulates an aversive response not only in the play's characters, but also in its spectators.

Modern neuroscientific study has confirmed the workings of this interaction between sufferer and spectator. Vittorio Gallese has observed how mirror neurons in the areas of the brain involved in pain processing fire in the same manner both when the individual performs a certain action and when the individual witnesses that action being performed (Gallese et al. 1996; Gallese and Goldman 1998). Consequently, the spectator can experience the sense of actively participating in the observed motion or physical state, and the reaction to such intense responsive feeling is frequently aversive, as Reyes observes:

> In the same way that the body in pain seeks relief so as to be able to function normally again, so the viewing body seeks to go back to its original state and conceal its viscerality and capacity for empathic feeling and sensation mimicry. (Reyes 2016: 177)

Pain studies thus understands the aversive response to pain, or to the sight of another's pain, as an evolutionary defence mechanism, a means of protecting the self from the threat of physical or even overwhelming emotional harm (Fields 2018: S3–4; De Peuter et al. 2011: 891). 'Signalling pain does not invariably lead to compassionate reactions' (Craig 2009: 27).

Waiting for Godot shares this perspective. In place of Schopenhauer's moralising, it prompts a more pragmatic understanding of pain as something we prefer to avoid. It is impossible to square Lois Gordon's assertion that, for Beckett, 'healing and caring are steadfast threads in the human fabric' (2013: 123) with the vision of his post-war play. Human beings are by no means incapable of offering compassion to their suffering fellow beings, *Waiting for Godot* tells us – but the response is not an instinctive one, and must be measured against one's own aversion to pain. The play's clear-eyed pragmatism is encapsulated in the exchange between Vladimir and Estragon, after Lucky has kicked Estragon:

> ESTRAGON: [*On one leg.*] I'll never walk again!
> VLADIMIR: [*Tenderly.*] I'll carry you. [*Pause.*] If necessary. (WG 32–3)

Vladimir's compassionate response is carefully, and comically, modulated by his own pragmatic self-interest. Selective reading has more typically emphasised sentences like Vladimir's 'To all mankind they were addressed, those cries for help still ringing in our ears! But at this place, at this moment of time, all mankind is us' (WG 74) as the moral heart of the play, without noting how such statements are immediately subjected to comic undercutting: only shortly after this pronouncement, for example, Vladimir will kick the distressed Pozzo in the attempt to silence his continued calls for help. In both textual emphasis and performance history, then, *Waiting for Godot* foregrounds how physical pain more typically stimulates an impulse to repudiation, rather than generating any affirmative communal experience.

Conclusion

Waiting for Godot enacts – both onstage and again in its auditorium – an instinctive human recoil from suffering, rather than any reassuring vision of a humanity united in redemptive shared feeling. Beckett's presentation of pain bears out medical and critical pain theory's understanding of how bodily suffering is typically an aversive and isolating phenomenon. The play does not offer any clear model of compassion as a means of relieving or redeeming a fellow being's distress. Rather, by delineating its characters' indifference to each other's pain, and by drawing the spectator's attention to her own impassivity and even recoil in the face of suffering, the play highlights just how narrow these bounds of human compassion seem to be. Simon Critchley has observed that Beckett's work undermines 'illusory narratives of redemption' and accentuates instead 'the profound limitedness of the human condition, of our frailty and separateness from each other' (2014: 211, 27). We might go still further. Returning to Beckett's own criticism of the 'redemptive perversion' of *Waiting for Godot* (LI 573), we note that he did not specify 'limitedness', 'separateness' or even 'frailty' as his vision for the play, but something 'nastier' (LI 611). It is 'nastiness' that is in large part bound up in the play's depiction of suffering.

The failure of the humanist reading of *Waiting for Godot* has been the refusal to accept this dimension of the play. There has been a critical resistance to acknowledging the play's vision of human nature as, at best, only precariously compassionate. *Waiting for Godot* demonstrates our instinctive aversion to pain and, like a symptom of the play's own diagnosis, the humanist reception demonstrates an aversion to this insight. Clinical pain studies helps us understand the aversive impulse as a fact rather than a failing. To instinctively recoil from the spectacle of suffering is not in itself a moral deficiency, and does not preclude the possibility of subsequent, rationalised compassion. *Waiting for Godot*'s exploration of pain – exposing the dark underside of humanist assumptions, yet counterbalanced with a comic pragmatism – scrutinises the necessary bounds of human compassion.

Chapter 6

'As if the sex matters': Beckett, Barthes and *Endgame* in Love

James Brophy

This essay reads *Endgame* beyond the normal interpretations posited in the fruitful critical ground between Beckett studies and queer studies, to ask what Beckett's queerness permits his work to do with sentimentality, and with love. Meanwhile I hope also to emphasise, in the second text that guides this exploration, Roland Barthes's *A Lover's Discourse: Fragments* (1978), the concept of a condition of 'an extreme solitude'. This is that space to which Barthes's lover, *l'amoureux*, is relegated, 'exiled from gregarity', from the socialised and normalised discursive realms (Barthes 1978: 2; hereafter LD). Love itself is an inherently queered and queering condition for Barthes's *amoureux*, and the world of Beckett's *Endgame* offers the grounds for a similar interrogation of love at its most essential and dialogic, with the specifics of gender and physical sexual acts set aside. Through Beckett and Barthes, I consider love's promise, its dialogic engagement, and its painful relation to endings. Barthes writes:

> *Reasonable* sentiment: everything works out, but nothing lasts.
> *Amorous* sentiment: nothing works out, but it keeps going on. (LD 140)

Barthes's contrasting of amorous with reasonable sentiment is telling: reason, here, depends upon the confirmation of sociality and of normality, a process of checking-in that the logic of love defies, indeed denies. What is quite literally radical about the queerness that pervades the world of Samuel Beckett's *Endgame* is that, in its carefully crafted extreme solitude, the heterosexual/homosexual binary is reduced to essentially nothing. Love itself, with its sentimental contours and catastrophic comforts, is presented as queered insofar as it is an investment and engagement that produces nothing beyond itself and cannot itself be abandoned. Love becomes, in this sense, corpsed (and, also, corpsing), which, Barthes suggests, is hardly unusual. The love of Barthes's exploration, of *l'amoureux*, always comes in this solitude it creates to rebound upon itself. Love must face the terror of itself, and it does so in the form of domestic set-pieces, so to speak, which Barthes calls the loverly 'figures'. These 'roles' into which the lover is at times 'stuffed' are 'established if at least someone can say, '"*That's so true! I recognize that scene of language!*"' (LD 4). The familiarity of such figures, audiences have long recognised, forms the foundation of Beckett's masterpiece. Take a step back, says Stanley Cavell, 'and they are simply a family' (1998: 60–1). Beckett told Alan Schneider that *Endgame* should 'be played as farcical parody of polite drawing-room conversation' (in Morin 2015: 61). In both cases, it is recognisable scenes of ordinary, idiomatic exchange that underpin, and generate, surreality. Beckett's uncanny play, like so much of his work, un-homes discourses of the home. His work demonstrates, under imposed conditions of solitude, qualities that are unseemly: for instance, the painful conflation of love's desperation and its pleasure. Beckett's is a kind of perverse defamiliarisation: rather than using literary techniques to allow one to see the beauty and possibility that has been made imperceptible by habit, he instead reveals things that are deeply unsettling, which wear habit so as not to be seen. In Barthes's discourse, within the exilic 'amorous life' it is the 'incredible futility' of the 'fabric of incidents . . . allied with the highest seriousness [that] is literally unseemly' (LD 178). This seems written to describe a Beckett play.

Behind much of Roland Barthes's work is a fantasy of a space beyond *doxa*, a space of what he called 'the neutral' where one gains respite from the tension between dichotomies that are demanded in the social world (1977b: 87). The space of *Endgame* is hardly that: instead of offering a peaceful resolution, it presents a dramatic escalation, even a *war zone*, defined by its lack of respite. As Mary F. Catanzaro puts it, '*Endgame* is a 24-hour study of combat habitat' (2007: 183). Beckett is recorded in the Haerdter rehearsal diaries of the Schiller Theater *Endspiel* as expressing much the same sentiment of the centrality of the dialogic battle: 'There must be maximum aggression between them from the first exchange of words onwards. Their war is the nucleus of the play' (in McMillan and Fehsenfeld 1988: 155). And yet, the battle is part of a war of attrition, as each is sapped of the will to carry on their combat: as they enact the scene of battle, each dissipates. This is what Barthes calls 'languor', an exhausting and oppressive inertia at the heart of the experience of *l'amoureux*, and inherent in the space of extreme solitude (LD 155).

I suggest that Beckett's *Endgame* has a lot more to do with love than readings of the play normally assume or permit; and that Barthes's *Lover's Discourse* has *less* to do with the love-life of ordinary language, because its love is a perceptively modern, queered condition that is an aspect of some, but certainly not all, experience. Love is not, for Barthes, a relation, so much as a private and socially deprived state. Together, these strange texts suggest something about the role, often difficult, that love can play as a force that persists parallel to its own languor. It drives neurotic impulses in both the play's central characters. For Hamm, it demands the obsessive project of the chronicle, and for Clov it energises a desperate fantasy for order. My reading emphasises the centrality of Clov's monologue, which we can read as being broken or interrupted by much of the action of the play, beginning with Hamm's awakening, and ultimately supplanted by Hamm's monstrously domineering chronicle. Hamm's first words, 'Me to play', as well as his terminal monologue (far more critically attended-to than Clov's), I argue, are interruptions and assertions of power that mirror aspects of love accounted for throughout Barthes's study. The dialogue of Hamm and Clov is less a chess game, as Kenner famously suggested (McMillan and Fehsenfeld 1988: 223), and more, in Barthes's phrase, 'a game of hunt-the-slipper [where] victory goes to the player who captures that little creature whose possession assures omnipotence: the last word' (LD 208). 'Hunt-the-slipper' is a Victorian-era parlour game where one tries to guess who is hiding an object that's been passed around a circle of seated players. It is the rough equivalent of 'jeu du furet' in Barthes's original (LD 247). While Hamm's chronicle engages in a domineering philosophising – 'Get out of here and love one another! Lick your neighbour as yourself!' (Beckett 2006b: 125; hereafter E1) – it is Clov's speech that offers what Barthes emphasises as 'the intractable', which he associates with a somewhat perverse affirmation: 'exiled from all gregarity, [the lover's discourse] has no recourse but to become the site, however exiguous, of an *affirmation*' (LD 1).

The degree to which, and the manner in which, queerness has been read into Beckett relates in part to the question of whether one takes his figures as paradigmatic universals (philosophical beings), or as contingent particulars (political beings). Emilie Morin has described the critical reception of *Endgame* in a context defined by the existentialism of 1950s French theatre more generally, in which Beckett's figures become 'representatives of humankind as a whole' (2015: 62). But this gives way as critics begin applying more historicising methods of interpretation. In order to offer insight into identity, critics ceased reading these characters as universals and began considering them as something like real people. Peter Boxall's work on queer Beckett points out that even as politically minded critics begin reading particularity into the characters – women read as women, Irish read as Irish – scholars have been 'slow to reflect upon the possibility that there might be an erotic dimension' to Beckett's male couples, even proposing an 'extraordinary demonstration of mass denial' regarding the issue (2004: 110). Boxall insists on recognising the legitimacy of reading sexual love into the oft-called 'pseudo-couples' of Beckett, attending to the 'sheer preponderance and centrality of homoerotic moments in Beckett's writing' (112). Yet this reassessment in which gay men be read as gay men perhaps has its own limits imposed by the dichotomy into which it makes its intervention. It's certainly true, as Catanzaro has pointed out, that Hamm 'exudes the air of the campy' (2007: 168), but with Barthes's deconstructive mode in mind, we find a potential for the queer that skirts the distinctions of a gay/straight binary. The characters can remain *queer* – in their same-sex relation, in their disability, in their lack of unselfconscious relation to a social world – but still *thereby* speak universally. The unresolved tension between queer and simply human, or of the queer experiencing the simply human, provides for a kind of attention all its own, neither purely philosophical nor exactly political (what of its politics could love retain in the corpsed world, in the exilic solitude?). This gay-but-not-gay-as-merely-gay dynamic is central to the success of Barthes's explicitly tacit, or tacitly explicit, discussion of same-sex love affairs in *A Lover's Discourse*.

The question of essential gayness was part of the early reception both of *Endgame* and *A Lover's Discourse*. Geoffrey Strickland's 1979 review of Barthes remarks that a reader is 'not always able to tell . . . whether the love in question is homosexual' and that 'we are clearly expected to concede that this is irrelevant' (1979: 72). Stanley Cavell's essay, written 1964, also brushes against the question of the play's homosexuality:

> I do not insist upon [Hamm and Clov's] appearing a homosexual relationship, although the title of the play just possibly suggests a practice typical of male homosexuality, and although homosexuality figures in the play's obsessive goal of sterility – the nonconsummation devoutly to be wished. (Cavell 1998: 62)

In Strickland, there is the contrary-to-fact conditional sense that the homosexual/heterosexual divide *is* relevant in love: he attempts to read-in the genders at play ('not *always* able to tell'). Cavell seems to want to evoke homosexuality between Clov and Hamm long enough to sustain two plays on words, both tellingly focused on physical erotics: 'Endgame' as a pun for anal sex, and nonconsummation as inherent in the version of sex typical of homosexuals. Both Strickland's winking acknowledgement about Barthes, and Cavell's about Beckett seem to me entirely wrongheaded (in addition to being problematic and *of their time*). What is essential in Barthes's text requires no such detective work: no specification of gender. And it seems clear that the homosexuality of *Endgame* does not inhere in physical erotic acts: indeed, the play is at pains to physicalise the lack of potential for sex, with Hamm who cannot stand and Clov who cannot sit, and Nell and Nagg relegated to their bins. The love explored in Barthes, and which I suggest *Endgame* interrogates on stage, is not relational, but to do with a condition. Queerness is not about male–male sex, for example, but is experiential and *individual*; and, banished from 'gregarity', beyond any remaining networks of normality, there is no social eye to label the queer. All love is queer in the corpsed world, and the love of which Barthes speaks always makes the world corpsed: unreal, or even disreal – an extreme solitude.

Physical erotic acts, like acts of violence, seem infinitely readable, theorisable and politically meaningful. The critic and director Herbert Blau is succinct in his own essay on Beckett and Barthes: 'For a time when all our thought, and certainly theory, seems infatuated with the sexual, love seems obscene' (2003: 94). Barthes makes much the same point: 'everyone will understand that X has "huge problems" with his sexuality; but no one will be interested in those Y may have with his sentimentality'; by contrast, love, for Barthes, 'is obscene precisely in that it puts the sentimental in place of the sexual' (LD 178). There is a specific critical ideology at play in mainstream queer studies, too, that has for a long time made it difficult to talk about love's sentimentality within its boundaries. A recent review by David Greven of a 2017 mainstream gay film demonstrates that even today there is an intervention to be staged on behalf of sentimentality against what Greven calls 'High Queer Theory'. Abandoning, or supplementing, attention to gay erotics, Greven wishes to attend to 'the idea of same-sex love', 'a bugbear for queer theory, which has cast it as a form of capitulation to and hapless imitation of heterosexual society' (2018: n.p.). Without romanticising queer suffering, contemporary queer theory might look to Beckett and Barthes who, I suggest, achieve insight about love by use of a not-specifically *gay*, but definitionally queer, exilic isolation: the experience of love they are able to depict and explore is hardly *lovely*, colloquially, but certainly worthy of theoretical attention. Barthes's 'lover', *l'amoureux*, is not simply one who is in love relationally – who dates, who marries – but he is the lover who suffers for his desire, one who experiences the love of Goethe's Werther, for example. He is a Romantic lover, a Petrarchan lover, a Platonic lover. Barthes's *amoureux* is not the lover *ordinaire*, but the lover who feels exquisitely and desperately, who persists in being in love independent of acts involving another, and who is common enough. He is the lover whose language, 'ignored, disparaged, or derided' is 'severed . . . from authority' and 'driven by its own momentum into the backwater of the "unreal"' (LD 1).

In order to extend this analysis, my reading of *Endgame* centres upon Clov's closing monologue:

CLOV: [*Fixed gaze, tonelessly, towards auditorium.*] They said to me, That's love, yes yes, not a doubt, now you see how – (E1 131–2)

Certain paradoxes that structure the play generally are to be found within this phrase, including the fact of its being cut off by Hamm's domineering 'Articulate!' These words offer a resonant metonym of the whole: *who* said to Clov that that's love? Of what matter or situation? What is the nature of Hamm's authority, extending even to Clov's very words? We might well read Clov as the son of the beseeching vassal of Hamm's chronicle; he is taken in as a boy to eventually become Hamm's 'son-servant-lover', in Cavell's phrasing (1998: 118). Who, though, is the 'they' that called this love? I will treat this monologue below, but having evoked 'That's love, yes yes, not a doubt', I want to account for the word 'love' more generally in the play.

The word in one form or another appears eleven times in *Endgame*. Two of its uses come in an early, telling interchange between Hamm and Clov:

HAMM: You don't love me.
CLOV: No.
HAMM: You loved me once.
CLOV: Once! (E1 95)

And another also closely borders on a nod towards the nature of their history together:

HAMM: I love the old questions. [*With fervour.*] Ah the old questions, the old answers, there's nothing like them! [*Pause.*] It was I was a father to you.
CLOV: Yes. [*He looks at HAMM fixedly.*] You were that to me.
HAMM: My house a home for you.
CLOV: Yes. [*He looks about him.*] This was that for me. (E1 110)

In two examples, 'love' is evoked in the English, though without the sense of *aimer* or *amour* in the French correlate. One is in Nell's first line, 'What is it, my pet? [*Pause.*] Time for love?' (E1 99), where the French makes use of a light and old-fashioned euphemism 'C'est pour la bagatelle?' (Beckett 1957: 27). Another comes when Hamm refers to the 'loveliness' of the sails of the fishing boats, long before Clov was 'in the land of the living' – in French, it is simply the boats' 'beauté' (E1 113; Beckett 1957: 31). Yet when Hamm, revelling in his ability still to *dream*, says, 'If I could sleep I might make love', we find in the French 'je ferais peut-être l'amour' (E1 100; Beckett 1957: 31). Another instance, Nagg's moving and bitter monologue, 'It's natural. After all I'm your father' (E1 119), finds him saying of Turkish Delight, 'there is nothing in the world I love more': 'je l'aime plus que tout au monde' (Beckett 1957: 74). Here is an instance Beckett could have easily used *like*, but gave to Nagg his own instance of 'love'. Tellingly, Nagg, who engages in the most touching and daily 'figures' of love – his enjoyment of a biscuit depending on Nell's having some, his crying for her when she dies – only actually utters the word 'love' when talking of Turkish Delight. He does get a lovely stage direction, at the end of his music-hall joke: 'and look – [*loving gesture, proudly*] – at my TROUSERS!' (E1 103). The direction's equivalent in *Fin de Partie* is, oddly, '[geste amoureux]', the French play's only use of Barthes's word for both lover and loverly (E1 103; Beckett 1957: 36).

The moments where love is spoken become dramatically emphasised, emboldened, both by its rarity in the play, and in contrast to the less serious or more idiomatic uses. There is, for example, of a crablouse, 'Catch him, for the love of God!'/'Attrape-la, pour l'amour du ciel!' (E1 108; Beckett 1957: 48). Physical love-making is banished to the realm of dreams alone, and procreation represents a dreadful fear, for it would only forestall the end of the languor (once more of the crablouse: 'humanity might start from there all over again!' (E1 108)). A few evocations of 'love' stand out as meaning something quite essential, quite powerful in this bleak world, neither merely idiomatic, nor (it would seem) ironic. The first is Hamm's love of the old questions, an impulse relating both to a dwelling in a past of his own narrative construction, and of continuing on through ritual pieces of interchange. The second, leaving aside Clov's speech for a moment longer, is his striking remark:

> CLOV: [*Straightening up.*] I love order. It's my dream. A world where all would be silent and still and each thing in its last place, under the last dust. (E1 120)

This pronouncement, 'J'aime l'ordre' in Beckett's French, recalls Barthes's own dream for order which strikes him *dans les ténèbres* during the dark nights in the figure 'Nuit'; here he speaks of being blinded by his attachment and the disorder, *désordre*, it brings (Beckett 1957: 76; Barthes 1977b: 203).

Clov's dream of order is also a dream of resolution, another central figure of the lover's obsessions of course; but order itself promises much to *l'amoureux* trapped in languor, as Barthes demonstrates in the section called 'Tutti sistemati' and filed under the term 'Casés', which Richard Howard's standard translation renders 'pigeonholed' (LD 45). As Hugh Kenner suggests of Clov's dream, 'Order is immobility, or else absence', a possibility for something like respite: a negative neutrality (1973: 125). It is in pursuit of order that Clov follows the rituals prescribed to him; he strives, in Barthes's terms, 'to enter a system', that is, 'a whole in which everyone has his place (even if it is not a good place); husband and wives, lovers, trios, marginal figures as well ... nicely installed in their marginality' (LD 45). Barthes at one point imagines the *amoureux* as one engaged in an existential game of *musical chairs* (not dissimilar to hunt-the-slipper: a game of concealment and exclusion), in which the one who remains 'standing' is the lover. Clov is quite literally the one who remains standing, desirous not of 'a union' (certainly not with Hamm, nor with anyone) (LD 46). What *l'amoureux* desires in the order he sees that excludes him, all things systematised (*tutti sistemati*) except him, is 'quite simply, a *structure*', for 'every structure is *habitable*', even if not happy: 'I can perfectly well inhabit what does not make me happy' (LD 46). Once more we see Barthes's *amoureux* is not in pursuit of a happy ending; he is in a condition of existential dread, defined not by its lack of *happiness*, but by a lack of *fitting-in*. It is, like Beckett's work pervasively, an exploration of a fundamental queerness which subsists in language, in banishment. Barthes offers a definition of the desire to be entered into a set identity within order, Clov's 'each thing in its last place': 'To want to be pigeonholed is to want to obtain for life a docile reception. As support, the structure is separated from desire: what I want, quite simply, is to be "kept," like some sort of superior prostitute' (LD 46). Elsewhere Barthes evokes the notion of the lover's realm as having 'perhaps ... no pleasure', but instead 'nothing but ... a frenzied activity of language' designed to institute 'the system (the paradigm) of demand and response' (LD 68).

The unfulfilled promise of order as a figure of *l'amoureux*'s desperation to escape his condition of solitude clearly explains Clov's entrapment in the house of Hamm: his servitude to the ritual is enough to sustain a desire for order. Yet he also remains the Barthesian lover, dreaming for the possibility of being encased (*casé*) in a systematic role 'for life', in Barthes's terms, 'under the last dust' in Clov's. Michael Haerdter's diaries describe Beckett's views on Clov's dream: 'a person creates his own world, *un univers à part*, to withdraw when one gets tired. . . in order to get away from the chaos into a simpler world' (in McMillan and Fehsenfeld 1988: 230). For Beckett, according to Haerdter, this desire for order is a crisis of the post-Enlightenment:

> The 18th century has been called the century of reason, *le siècle de la raison*. I've never understood that: they're all mad, *ils sont tous fous, ils déraisonnent*! They give reason a responsibility which it simply can't bear, it's too weak. (Haerdter, in McMillan and Fehsenfeld 1988: 230–1)

Beckett's remarks suggest that Clov's dream isn't for the confirmation of a socially situated security – his dream of order is, oddly, the dream of a private space. Beckett's remarks are quite turned around: the horror he's created for Clov and Hamm is precisely *un univers à part*, and the torment is, already, *withdrawal*. Clov's dream of order is the Barthesian desire to escape the solitude, to see 'all that order', that beauty, that would mark a return to sociality (now gone and beyond recovery). Barthes describes at one point the 'lover's fatal identity' as '*the one who waits*': an indeterminacy manifests that neither wants to go, nor can stay: the lover standing at the door, like the moment before the end of Ibsen's famous play (LD 40). Barthes describes a different figure, that of the '*issues*', the 'outcomes' as being 'like the pregnant moment . . . of bourgeois drama: sometimes this is a farewell scene' (LD 143).

If Clov's governing 'figure' is that of the dream of submission within order, for Hamm it is surely a dream of control. As Barthes describes in his 'fading', or 'fade-out', section: 'love is' at times, 'monologic, maniacal' (LD 112). Indeed, Barthes defines the very *dis-*

cours amoureux as 'my little sacred history that I declaim to myself' (LD 94). Hamm's sacred history is, unlike Barthes's, emphatically *not* for himself alone, but takes on a tyrannical aspect of the 'monstrous discourse'. In the section called 'monstreux/monstrous', Barthes investigates the figure of the *discours amoureux* turned tyrannical – the lover 'has been pitiable, now he becomes monstrous' (LD 165). Hamm will demand, or certainly prefer, an audience to witness his suffering ('can there be misery – [*he yawns*] – loftier than mine?') in the form either of his servant Clov or of his cursed progenitor, Nagg (E1 93). Hamm compels Clov-as-auditor into the figure of 'dependency', of which Barthes blithely remarks, 'the mechanics of amorous vassalage require a fathomless futility' (LD 82). 'It's we who are obliged to each other' Hamm tells Clov just before Hamm's ultimate narrative, confirming the complementary aspect of their particular loverly figures (E1 132).

Hamm's domineering narrative, broken into two extended portions, is itself of the history of his domination. Its central plot (at least on the day we observe Hamm and perhaps every day) is to do with the 'extra-ordinarily bitter day', on which a man comes to beg food and shelter for 'himself and the child' (E1 117). These details are revealed to an audience consisting of Nagg, bribed with the promise of a sugarplum; at the very end of the play, Hamm continues the narrative to an audience consisting (though he doesn't know it) of Clov, poised at the door 'dressed for the road' (E1 132). In the final moments of his chronicle, he sarcastically reiterates the man's wish, 'If he could have his child with him . . .', before revealing, 'It was the moment I was waiting for': the moment being an opportunity to berate the father for the irresponsibility of wanting to prolong a child's life – 'You ought to know what the earth is like, nowadays'! (E1 133.) Barthes describes the lover's compositions, his language, his writing, as 'a kind of steamroller [that] would kill "father, mother, lover" rather than deviate from its frailty' (LD 78). Barthes recognises, as we the audience recognise in Hamm's chronicle, that for the lover 'there is no benevolence within writing, rather a terror: it smothers the other, who, far from perceiving the gift in it, reads there instead an assertion of mastery, of power, of pleasure, of solitude' (LD 78–9). We also recognise, importantly, that such killing, smothering, monstrosity relates to an essential and deeply pathetic frailty in Hamm. Hamm's narrative impulse issues from a haemorrhage that he associates with an artery, a pulsating 'heart, a heart in [his] head'; the stage curtain finds its symbolic counterpart famously in the stauncher that Hamm wears on his face when he sleeps to collect the blood that presumably comes out his mouth or nose (E1 100). Barthes recognises this sense of slow dissipation '[i]n amorous languor', this 'something [that] keeps going away' and even suggests that it is 'as if desire were nothing but this hemorrhage' (LD 156).

Clov and Hamm offer complementary aspects, then, of *l'amoureux*, who 'hesitate[s] between tyranny and oblation' (LD 42). Barthes describes this duality, this hesitancy, in the section he calls 'Dark Glasses', filed under the figure of *cacher*, or 'to hide'. The dark, obscuring sunglasses for Barthes are a kind of habit, a kind of veil, as if worn in mourning, which defines in part the parameters of his unreal, exiled existence. Hamm, whom we are told is to wear black glasses, accesses an important potential from this veil – it permits the lover to hide in various senses: 'hide from the other how much I love him?' perhaps; 'I see the other with a double vision: sometimes as object, sometimes as subject' (LD 42). The glasses permit the lover to enact his wish of being at once 'both pathetic and admirable', at once 'a child and an adult' (LD 42). This is a mode of 'cunning preterition', that at all moments permits him to express himself purely linguistically: the dark glasses remove the body, which, according to Barthes, foils language's desire to 'do everything: even and especially [to] *say nothing*' (LD 43, 44). In Barthes, the body, and particularly the lover's eyes, say: 'I am a liar . . . not an actor' but hidden behind his glasses, behind which Clov claims never to have peeked, Hamm can uphold Beckett's beloved irresolvability: be at once liar and actor (LD 44).

Hamm and Clov's complementarity, that they are 'merely aspects of a single consciousness, vital spirits mingling within the conarium', is a reading 'many have observed' (Ackerley and Gontarski 2004: 177). It is also commonly observed that '*Endgame* is a play about a play': an actor trapped in the horror of playing out before an audience that which never concludes (177). Among Barthes's lengthiest and most explored figures is that of the *scène*, as when a couple *makes a scene*, whether publicly or privately. This ritual enacting scene making is for Barthes the 'exercise of a right, the practice of a language of which they are co-owners' (LD 204). The figure of the scene deletes, to some degree, the difference between sharing a stage and sharing a consciousness: it is a game of which both parties know full well the terrain and the stakes. Clov's attempts, however sincere, to leave prompt Hamm at one point to describe 'the dialogue' of which the two are co-owners (for Hamm has taught Clov his words, we have learned):

CLOV: I'll leave you.
HAMM: No!
CLOV: What is there to keep me here?
HAMM: The dialogue. [*Pause.*] I've got on with my story. [*Pause.*] I've got on with it well. [*Pause. Irritably.*] Ask me where I've got to. (E1 120–1)

Of the *scène*, the 'set exchange of remarks' defined by a 'view to having the "last word"', Barthes says it is only 'euphemistically called *dialogue*' (LD 204); Hamm immediately demands of Clov that he ask how his chronicle is proceeding. True dialogue would necessitate the return to a (burgeoning) sociality, while Hamm perversely desires to remain in the solitude of his Barthesian *amoureux*, or at least doesn't know how it might be moved beyond. 'Monologue', Barthes continues, is 'pushed back to the very limits of humanity', a condition shared by the 'proto-actor, the madman, and the lover', certainly adequate descriptions of Hamm (LD 204–5).

For Barthes, the scene is impelled forward by that desire to have the last word, for to have the finality of that last word is to 'assign destiny to everything that has been said, is to master, to possess, to absolve' (LD 208). It is, furthermore, nothing short of the ability 'to bludgeon meaning': 'in the space of speech, the one who comes last occupies a sovereign position' (LD 208). Hamm, the fallen lord of language, belated, down to his last vassal, maintains that sovereignty by having the last word before returning beneath his stauncher. Appropriately, it is just before this interruption that we get Beckett's own attempt to define love, his own commentary on (however exiguous) love:

CLOV: [*Fixed gaze, tonelessly, towards auditorium.*] They said to me, That's love, yes yes, not a doubt, now you see how – . . . How easy it is. They said to me, That's friendship, yes yes, no question, you've found it. They said to me, Here's the place, stop, raise your head and look at all that beauty. That order! They said to me, Come now, you're not a brute beast, think upon these things and you'll see how all becomes clear. And simple! They said to me, What skilled attention they get, all these dying of their wounds.
. . .
I say to myself – sometimes, Clov, you must learn to suffer better than that if you want them to weary of punishing you – one day. I say to myself – sometimes, Clov, you must be there better than that if you want them to let you go – one day. But I feel too old, and too far, to form new habits. Good, it'll never end, I'll never go. [*Pause.*] Then one day, suddenly, it ends, it changes, I don't understand, it dies, or it's me, I don't

understand that either. I ask the words that remain – sleeping, waking, morning, evening. They have nothing to say. [*Pause*.] I open the door of the cell and go. I am so bowed I only see my feet, if I open my eyes, and between my legs a little trail of black dust. I say to myself that the earth is extinguished, though I never saw it lit. [*Pause*.] It's easy going. [*Pause*.] When I fall I'll weep for happiness. (E1 131–2)

This speech is little attended to in Beckett studies. It receives no close attention, for example, in any of the essays in Mark Byron's volume (2007). Andrew Gibson, though, does make it a focus in his summative conclusion to *The Pathos of Intermittency*. Gibson's concept of intermittency, or that quality 'generated in the gap between events and their remainder' (1996: 23) that is both the 'negative of *jouissance*' and its repressed 'shadowy corollary' (257), is crystallised in Clov's speech. He describes it as 'at once bracingly and witheringly sardonic', and explains that it draws us in, '[f]or all our bafflement', with 'the sheer power of the phrasing at such moments' (256). This reading of Clov's speech, as antithesis of the pleasures of *jouissance*, is substantiated by Beckett's directorial notes that it is about the '"five dispensers of life's consolation", love, friendship, nature, science, and mercy' (in Gibson 1996: 256). That 'that beauty. That order' refers to nature, and 'All becomes clear' names science, seems comparatively unconvincing, Beckett's notes aside. The play, and this speech, are certainly more about love than those other dispensers of life's consolation, it seems to me. Through Barthes, we elect love to a primary position – 'that's love' is powerfully striking in its simplicity as a statement. Barthes's own sense of *jouissance* as the powerful bliss that comes with the detonation of expected codes certainly seems, as Gibson finds through Badiou, a convincing and informative antithesis to what I suggest we in fact find in Clov's speech: the languor of love's desire.

It *is* love that Clov speaks of: a punishing condition that, as he says at the very start of the play, 'must be nearly finished', but which does not finish – until: 'One day, it ends, it changes, I don't understand, it dies, or it's me' (E1 132). What strikes me about this monologue, this offering from Clov's heart to Hamm's demand, is, as with Gibson, its beauty of articulation: its supreme power as a monologue, perhaps one of the greatest of contemporary theatre. In the section called 'The World Thunderstruck', Barthes describes the immense power of the mastery of language. He describes extreme solitude as oscillating between the difficult states of the *unreal* and the unutterable *disreal*, which he also thinks of as a kind of death. Of linguistic mastery, he describes, 'Yet if I can manage . . . to *utter* this death, I begin to live again; I can posit antitheses, release exclamations' (LD 91). Must we read 'when I fall I'll weep for happiness' as defeat? Rather, the beauty of Clov's speech itself is what it declares itself to be, 'That's love' (E1 131).

While Hugh Kenner's early and influential readings of Beckett declared that 'Behind work after work of Beckett's we are to sense a loss, somewhere in the past, of the power to love', of *Endgame*, in particular, he writes: 'We need not add that theirs is a loveless world' (1973: 15, 125). And yet, through Barthes's sense of love as an isolated form of modern experience, a queered and queering perspective that calls up the solipsistic world-unto-itself, we can recognise that love persists importantly, maybe definitionally, in Beckett's world. It is the lover as 'one who waits', the lover as 'one who remains', as Hamm remains (LD 41, 13). If there were no love, there would be no pity. 'What goes by the name of love is banishment', Beckett writes in *First Love*, 'with now and then a postcard from the homeland' (1995: 31). This exilic love brings us, I think, again and again to his work for its depictions of those familiar scenes, those 'figures' of intimacy so troublingly exiled: so extreme in their solitude. Endings, the obsession of Beckett's masterwork, are also an obsession of Barthes's study of love. In each, they are that which both defines the ongoing condition, and which cannot be accounted for by it. Love, as the isolated condition, can only replicate, start again, because of a definitional constraint of the lover's discourse: that 'I myself cannot . . . construct my love story to the end' (LD 101). Like Hamm, the Barthesian *amoureux* is the 'poet . . . only for the beginning; the end, like my own death, belongs to others' (LD 101). Barthes's discussion often turns towards the theatrical and, indeed, we all intuit the experience of love as a dramatic one: a deeply performative one. *A Lover's Discourse* helps us to see the fatigue, the languor, of it, and *Endgame*, though a short, one-act, play, accomplishes the feat of making us *feel* that oppressive languor. 'There is a scenography of waiting', a miming of the 'loss [and] all the effects of a minor mourning', Barthes explains, 'This is then acted out as a play' (LD 37).

I end with a reflection on Nell and Nagg. These parents of Hamm are most inarguably lovers, and supremely sentimental and moving in their attachment and dedication to one another, degraded though they've become. However, these characters are emphatically, demonstrably, *not* lovers of Barthes's exilic kind, of the discourse of extreme solitude. Having come as a pair, a couple, into this queered after-world, this site of exiguous affirmations, they share a history of before: memories of the Ardennes, old jokes, an ongoing if pitiful affection. Yes, they are pitiable and degraded – a degradation that feeds Hamm's amorous desire for dominance – but they are not in the position of endlessness; their lot is not one condemned to an end that cannot be written. Nell does find an end, it seems, in dying; and Nagg finds his end in his wife's demise. They are not soliloquists like Hamm, which permits Nagg to curse his son by wishing that one day Hamm will lack the audience that confirms him. After Nell's death, Nagg is found crying; this is more than either Clov or Hamm is ever able to do – this is an end to an old and ultimately difficult marriage, but a marriage nonetheless and not a love affair. For the Barthesian lovers Hamm and Clov, by contrast, 'the idea of outcome adjusts itself to the foreclosure of any outcome: the lover's discourse is in a sense a series of No Exists' (LD 142). 'This', Barthes writes of the loverly exile, 'is an extreme theater. Whence the awkwardness – or, for some perverse types, the pleasure' (LD 123).

Chapter 7

Beckett's Queer Time of *Défaillance*: Ritual and Resistance in *Happy Days*

Nic Barilar

When he was in rehearsals directing Billie Whitelaw for the 1979 production of *Happy Days* (1961) at London's Royal Court Theatre, Beckett said of Winnie, 'She's not stoic, she's unaware' (Beckett 1985: 17). But, unaware of what, exactly? James Knowlson interprets this to mean that she is 'largely unaware of the sad realities of her situation', but notes that, under Beckett's direction, Whitelaw played Winnie on the edge of madness, with flashes of despair that hinted she sensed death's creeping approach (15–17). Beckett's Winnie is more aware of her situation than Knowlson suggests. She acknowledges that she's stuck in the ground (Beckett 2013: 30–1, 35–6, 40, 44–5, 63, 68; hereafter HD). She is acutely aware of the ear-splitting bell that tells her when to wake up and go to sleep (HD 37, 46, 48, 59, 62, 64). Neither is she immune to or unaware of pain (HD 14, 47, 59, 65). In his production notes, Beckett made a list of what he called '*Défaillances*' that Whitelaw performed as 'moments of weakness' when Winnie 'becomes intermittently aware of her situation and closest to breakdown' (1985: 138). If Winnie remains unaware of anything, it's the futility of her actions. Rather, she contrives to remain in ignorance, but fails in that, too.

This complicates the evaluations of critics, like Jennifer M. Jeffers, who note Winnie's 'British Victorian society values of self-restraint and righteous suffering' (2009: 141). With its frantic emotional and physical contrasts (Beckett 1985: 15), Whitelaw's manic take rather magnifies Winnie's failure to exemplify the 'British pluck' that critics, actors and directors see in her. If played stoically, Winnie's determination in the face of insurmountable suffering recuperates her failure as success, and makes her routines a means to an end that she awaits with patient endurance. Yet, Winnie does not embrace death in the short or long term. She neither shoots herself with the revolver nor calmly accepts her fate. Incapable of ignoring the bell's regimentation of her life, as she admits in act two (HD 59–60), she has a choice: do nothing, or do something – and she refuses to sit idly by (HD 29). Instead, she avoids the tedium of an empty present by filling it with domestic rituals – applying make-up, speaking to her husband – which allow her to pace her day. In doing so, she seeks to put the encroaching entropy out of her mind but, whatever she does, she cannot escape her dilemma. Each time she manages to get swept up in busyness, Beckett has her fail. This is the 'sorrow [that] keeps breaking in', as Winnie calls it (HD 36), which punctures her 'profound frivolity' (Beckett 1985: 17). When the bell chimes, when she runs out of things to say, is reminded of her age, or of time's progress, Winnie's personal *longue durée* confronts her (and her audience) again.

For example, early in the play, she spends considerable time labouring to read the inscription on her toothbrush's handle. After she pulls a pair of spectacles from her bag, she attempts to read the text again, fails again, cleans her glasses, takes another shot, fails yet again, cleans the handle itself, and tries once more before admitting defeat (HD 13–15). Beckett altered the end of this sequence for the 1979 production. Rather than lay down the objects, as both the published English and French texts dictate, Beckett had Whitelaw arrest the gesture as she says, 'Old things. [*Pause.*] Old eyes. [*Long pause.*] On, Winnie' (HD 15; Beckett 1974: 17; 1985: 162). This alteration is telling. The arrested gesture embodies a correction whereby she shifts the blame from the old objects to her own old eyes. Here, Winnie recognises the passage of time and it produces in her an interruption so profound she must literally urge herself onwards.

In Beckett's production, this disturbance comes on the heels of Winnie's first *défaillance* (Beckett 1985: 45). As she cleans her toothbrush, Winnie reflects that she doesn't experience much pain beyond the occasional migraine which 'comes [...] then goes' (HD 14). Whitelaw drew out the rhythm of her polishing, eventually came to a pause, lowered her head, and 'brokenly' intoned, 'prayers perhaps not for naught' (HD 14; Beckett 1985: 162). If her headaches pass, Winnie must concede that time also passes, hence change is inevitable. Throughout, she is at pains to keep change at bay, repeating her mantra: 'No better, no worse, no change' (HD 12, 15). In her prayers, too: 'World without end Amen' (HD 11). Here, Beckett suggests that Winnie wants to resist time itself. She longs for perpetuity, but the *défaillance* points up the impossibility inherent in that desire. The pressures of time compel her to get back to the busyness that allows her to cope. And while these acts distract her, they do nothing to defeat degeneration, stall time, or free her from her slow entombment in the earth. Beckett assaults his audience, and his characters, with the fact that resistance fails: time keeps ticking.

Recent studies have nuanced our understanding of Beckettian time. Eric P. Levy argues that Beckett's temporality is forward moving and typified by repetition in a way that 'simply reiterates sameness' (2011: 92). Michelle Chiang critiques this view, seeing Beckett's characters as caught in a struggle between dual temporalities (2018: 100). For Chiang, Beckett's characters live between intuitive time and an imposed time shaped by external habits (3–9). In this reading, external time oppresses its internal counterpart (95, 104). Chiang goes further, claiming this split temporality also affects the audience, putting them back in touch with their intuitive centre (6). Chiang qualifies this observation, however, recognising that the audience never completely gives over to the spectacle (155). In *Happy Days*, Beckett enacts and emphasises this separation by way of the bell. However jarring it might be for them, the audience exists beyond the bell's demands. The bell acts on Winnie, and the audience experiences time according to how well she copes with it. When she fails, or when the bell rings in the second act, the audience members fall out of sync with her.

This division points to a dynamic not fully appreciated in Beckett studies: audiences bring their own temporality into the theatre. There are multiple temporalities at any given performance, and audiences can oscillate between them. According to Chris Morash and Shaun Richards, an audience will typically experience theatrical time as duration, but can approach, be brought into, be separated from, or distance themselves from the temporality performed onstage (2013: 94–6). Unlike reading, where the reader can stop, go make a cup of tea, and choose when to return to the text, theatre entails a kind of entrapment, and Beckett consciously exploits this feature of performance. As Stanton B. Garner, Jr. argues, theatre begs its audience for investment because it is a mutually constitutive act of world building: 'spectacle is set into motion by our gaze – we sanction this being-present through our applause, our laughter, even the attentiveness of our silence' (1994: 49). Beckett might encourage us to add 'our shuffling in our seats' to the list. When Winnie is able to distract herself, the audience is more distracted as well. Winnie pulls the audience along with her, catching them in her temporal net, and they hail her in return: 'Someone is looking at me still. [*Pause*] Caring for me still', she says at the top of the second act (HD 55). However, when she inevitably fails, when a *défaillance* happens,

Beckett opens an affective/temporal rupture between audience and character.

In *Happy Days*, Winnie alternates between recognition of her failure and assertions of 'normalcy'. Each time she fails, and becomes aware of her situation, her sense of changeless time falters. This pattern helps to establish identification with the audience. With each step of the pattern, the audience is moved to empathy. When Winnie's failure is most evident, the audience feels her failure as an affective, negative temporality. When time is out of joint it's uncomfortable. Seeing and feeling Winnie fail makes the audience hope she can get back up and fight again, futile as that fight may be. Stuck with Winnie in the theatre, the audience asks, 'What else can I do?' The play works to normalise the audience's response while leaving just enough space in the gap opened up by the split time of the *défaillance* to (only maybe) provide some critical distance; a space from which to evaluate the affective pull of what they are witnessing. Beckett triangulates Winnie's predicament through her audience and manipulates them by metatheatrical means. Further, the audience's prurient gaze implicates them as voyeurs of her predicament. In this way, it becomes possible to understand certain elements of the play's dramaturgy (e.g. time, the body, the audience) as configurations of historical understanding, and even models of the political itself.

Queer studies has advanced theories of time as an oppressive force that can help to illuminate Beckett's method. Jack Halberstam (2005) argues that the logic of late capitalism choreographs the normative sequence of life's events from unruly childhood to disciplined adulthood through education, marriage, property acquisition, parenthood: the very cycle that secures the reproduction of family and/as nation. The logic of late capitalism, he argues, prompts an 'early to bed, early to rise' mentality that merges the *mythos* of capitalist success with notions of time-well-spent. Guilt hovers over leisure while productivity is always a virtue. Halberstam maintains that this capitalist temporality is predicated upon heterosexual, monogamous reproduction, and names 'queer time' any temporal deviation from it (2005: 1–8). Queer time offers different logics, social arrangements and identities to 'straight time' (Pryor 2017: 4), to what Elizabeth Freeman terms 'chrononormativity': 'the interlocking temporal schemes necessary for [. . .] the mundane workings of domestic life' (2010: xxii). It is an aspect of what Michel Foucault terms 'biopower', the governmental mechanisms that regulate 'life and the biological processes of man-as-species', from procreation to thought (2003: 246–7; 1991). Chrononormativity structures and perpetuates biopower in its normalising effects, organising and manipulating disciplinary time to seem 'natural'. If straight time props up such 'regimes of the normal' (Warner 1993: xxvi), queerness might serve to resist such regimes. At stake is the liberating potential of queer ways of being and knowing to provide a release from the burdens of dutiful, chrononormative existence.

In *Happy Days*, however, Beckett queers theatre's salvific potential, querying, in turn, how liberating queer time might be. Beckett saw how productions of *Waiting for Godot* (1955) tended towards what he called a 'redemptive perversion': people couldn't help but see a glimmer of solace in his bleak vision (LII 573). This optimism is also discernible in performance studies, where, according to Jaclyn I. Pryor, 'negative affects are difficult to maintain' (2017: 16). For Pryor, 'theater, dance, and performance are, arguably, inherently acts of hope' (16). This is difficult to believe where Beckett is concerned. Where queer and feminist scholars like Pryor, Jill Dolan (2005) and José Muñoz (2009) credit theatre with an ability to produce and sustain alterity through an intersubjective process of meaning making, Beckett stages the processes that normalise violence and perpetuate suffering. He uses theatrical time not so much to build community as to underscore its complicity with oppression. In his brilliant monograph on Beckett's aesthetics, James McNaughton shows how Beckett's plays utilise theatrical form to model political coercion as, for example, in *Play* (1964), where the spotlight acts like an interrogator, prompting the characters to speak. In his brief reading of *Happy Days*, McNaughton reads Winnie's entombment as a metatheatrical commentary on how 'passivity toward individual suffering and historical catastrophe has been democratized' (2018: 90). In this way, *Happy Days* testifies to the violent processes of normalisation that structure and limit Winnie's life. Where utopian thinkers like Dolan, Muñoz and Pryor see theatre and performance's capacity to map and forge new kinship relations and feel a more perfect future in the imperfect present, Beckett turns these dynamics inside out and upside down to queer or question the ethics and norms of theatrical participation itself. For if, as McNaughton puts it, 'Theatrical space models political power so aptly because political power aspires to theatrical possibility' (2018: 90), Beckett uses the empathetic engines of temporal identification to model how theatre induces audiences to partake in the normalisation of suffering and violence.

That said, the redemptive interpretation is very difficult to resist in the embodied space of the theatre. McNaughton's insight into how Beckett fuses dramaturgy, stagecraft and history in an aesthetic politics is invaluable. He takes seriously Beckett's injunction about the catastrophe of history and the failures of modernism to its logical and radical extremes. However, he overlooks the role of time, and how it complicates Beckett's aesthetic/political project. Following Morash and Richards, we might say, Beckett's audience comes into the space with their own sense of time, one that syncs with Winnie's as she sets her pace. Then Beckett manipulates the onstage situation so that they slip in and out of sync with her. As Winnie copes, so does the audience. They come to share her sense of the present based on an identification with the chrononormative imperative to act 'productively' – to 'make use of their time'. But when the *défaillances* happen, Beckett interrupts this process of identification, exposing its shallow nature. By making the audience share Winnie's embodied chrononormative experience, Beckett renders the slips and jolts out of the drudgery of straight time, into the listless negativity of queer time, palpable. But he also shows how complicity is created, using theatre as a model. The audience is made to identify-then-dissociate from Winnie's plight as a function of self-comfort. Even as her *défaillances* make this disjunction discernible, they also reinforce the normal time of the theatre. The drudge suddenly seems more bearable. The sharing of temporal affect, as Morash and Richards argue, depends upon the degree of identification between audience and character, which means that in order for spectators to approach temporal synchronisation, Beckett must keep one foot planted in realism. The audience, meanwhile, can keep one eye on the exit.

Happy Days shares much in common with dramas of domestic and marital estrangement. For as much as they are a reaction against realism, as Garner argues, Beckett continues to rely 'on an autonomous, physicalized *mise-en-scène* that serves to both enable and to constrain the actions conducted within it' (1994: 103). For Jeffers, Winnie is a symbol of dying social traditions that somehow continue to go on (2009: 143), but this also includes some of the conventions of realism. Beckett splinters the singular, affective temporality characteristic of that form, but retains its identifying effects precisely in order to critique the theatrical, embodied ethics of aesthetic coercion – which, itself, responds to normalising and political histories. And while Winnie fails spectacularly, Beckett charts a rather different relationship between time, failure and queerness than what has emerged as the dominant statement on failure in queer theory. Halberstam's *The Queer Art of Failure* (2011) characterises queerness as particularly marked by failure, itself the negative outcome of a world driven by the success market. Halberstam claims that 'Failure is something queers do and have always done exceptionally well'; is a way to 'escape the punishing norms that discipline behavior and manage human development' (2011: 3). Halberstam grounds his readings for the most part in family-friendly animated films that offer a popular if silly archive of covertly queer possibilities (20). Halberstam is invested in reading representations of queer failure as revolution or resistance, an impetus that grows from Leo Bersani's claim that 'gay desire' entails 'a revolutionary inaptitude for heterotized sociality' (1995: 7).

By Halberstam's own admission, though, such media rarely permit the representations they contain to follow through on their potential. They almost always end happily ever after with little or no change to the status quo. The value, Halberstam argues, is in following the bad things that happen along the way and owning them (2011: 186–7). While Halberstam's analyses offer a trenchant defence of forgetting, naïvety, stupidity and losing as alternative methods of knowing and being, by situating his examples in mass-consumer media that end 'happily' and couching failure as revolution or resistance, he often recuperates failure as another pathway to success. In a way, Winnie fits quite nicely into Halberstam's cast of 'losers' in the stoic or 'British' reading of *Happy Days*. However, her routines don't amount to revolution or resistance against regimes of the normal, but actually bolster them, making a virtue of necessity with the limited tools available to her. If anything, she resists the queer potential of the temporalities she inhabits. And it's not that she has no choice. The bell doesn't demand she do anything at all but wake or sleep when it rings. It is Winnie's choice to fill that time with activity, because to do nothing is unbearable. Yet, straight time fails her over and over again. Her routines may feel like successful resistance (so much so that she makes the audience feel the same way through their temporal affect), but they simply offer ways to cope with entrapment. Beckett takes his audience to the limits of failure-as-resistance through an embodied meditation on the disciplining forces of regulative regimes of the normal. By enacting resistance to straight time as failure, and by refusing to see failure itself as queer time, Beckett creates an interpretive structure in which seeing any redemption in Winnie's actions risks complicity with the violence of chrononormative structures.

The play's bell is a key feature of the dramaturgy and Winnie is at its mercy, a crucial choice Beckett made in revision when he changed what was first an alarm clock Winnie kept onstage to set her own pace (Gontarski 2017: 37–8). Without that kind of control over time, Winnie uses ritual and routine to pace her day. These have their own affective temporality, and it is the effect of domesticated temporality that she seeks. The bell forces Winnie to normalise her abnormal scenario, using everyday rituals to divert her attention from the horror of her situation. What feels best to her are those actions which skirt the abnormality of her life. Her routines are themselves bound to normalising, gendered regimes of straight time that demarcate her possibilities. As historian Deana Heath argues, when the middle classes emerged they cultivated hegemonic standards based on an idealised domesticity that restricted the bourgeois body and defined respectability (2010: 37). Such practices buttressed and enacted normalisation, participated in capitalism, projected success, and endorsed humdrum routine as necessary for maintaining the status quo. The logic of straight time undergirds this repertoire and constructs this logic as natural rather than imposed, masking its psychic and physical violence. In *Happy Days*, Beckett rips off the mask and exposes that violence, but also makes the audience take part in it.

The play ties domesticity and commodity culture to chrononormativity. Winnie constantly turns to her bag and the objects it contains as well as her husband, Willie, to maintain her preferred, busy temporality. Her toothpaste, medicine and lipstick cue temporal meanings as they are running low, a fact she says that 'can't be helped' (HD 12) because the moment necessitates their use. The bag is especially useful to her as a pacing tool: 'Do not overdo the bag, Winnie, make use of it of course, let it help you . . . along, when stuck, by all means, but cast your mind forward, Winnie, to the time when words must fail' (HD 34). After her parasol bursts into flames and she throws it away, she comments that it will return to her side the next day (HD 39, 41). She hurls the mirror over her shoulder as well, claiming it, too, will return (HD 41). Here, Winnie again strives for continuity and changelessness. She discards her possessions but immediately recognises her dependency upon them. She can't quite convince herself that things won't change, but it's better to keep going than to dwell on the time. Her attempts at sustaining normalcy rely just as much upon her connection to Willie as upon her objects. In fact, it is only after Willie interacts with her that she declares it to be 'Another happy day!' (HD 17, 25, 41, 49, 69). She even suggests that without her husband she would have nothing to do and no reason to speak:

> Whereas if you were to die [. . .] or go away and leave me, then what would I do, what *could* I do, all day long, I mean between the bell for

waking and the bell for sleep? [...] Not another word as long as I drew breath, nothing to break the silence of this place. [*Pause.*] Save possibly, now and then, every now and then, a sigh into my looking-glass. (HD 23)

Later in the play, when she is buried up to her neck, she confesses that she has not heard from Willie in a long time, and is not certain he is still there or even alive (HD 56). Not knowing whether or not Willie remains allows her to continue speaking because, by her own logic, there is little use in talking to herself (even if that's actually what she's already doing anyway) (HD 57). This thought experiment demonstrates both Winnie's commitment to performing domesticity as a way to normalise her life as well as her inability to entertain any other way of living – a violence that nevertheless safeguards her against the queer temporal field she so adamantly resists.

Such normalising regimes commit violence against those who participate in them, and Beckett locates this violence in Winnie's commitment to her banal activities. For Beckett, the dull routines of the 'normal' day-to-day are a form of violence. He understood how this worked thanks to his encounters with the Irish state's normalising project (Morin 2009: 40–5; Kennedy 2010; Stewart 2011: 50–6). Even before the horrors of World War II showed the atrocious lengths to which biopower could go, Beckett understood the violence inherent in normalisation. In *Happy Days*, he enacts the insidiousness of this process. If, as McNaughton argues, *The Unnamable* (1958) satirises 'regulated capitalism', asking 'whether the logic of capital extraction might find it expedient to eliminate the unproductive' (2018: 114), in *Happy Days*, Winnie's domesticated productivity leads only to distraction while time ticks on.

Like Winnie's appeal to her objects, her connection with Willie has its limits. Indeed, it is often her conversations with Willie that produce her *défaillances* – a problem she is aware of but unable to address. At one moment, Willie refuses to cooperate with her, causing her to recognise the threadbare nature of their relationship. This interrupts her illusion of domesticity and so she distracts herself, commenting on her painful confinement (HD 30–1). Coupling her awareness of the mound, the ultimate symbol of her precarity, with dialogue that lays bare the frailty of her union with Willie, brings her to an awareness of the limits of domestic rituals to sustain her. It also disrupts the audience's identification with her. When she comes to stillness and enters queer time in the *défaillance*, the audience enters their own distanced and uneasy temporal space. What a relief, then, for the theatregoers, that Winnie re-establishes a connection with

Willie by turning a common ant, which happens to be passing by, into something humorously novel. Just like that, distraction takes hold and returns Winnie to willed normalcy, and the audience can also get back to passing the time with Winnie, if not outright enjoying her dangerous frivolity.

Beckett's critique is grounded in and responds to history. France, Great Britain and Ireland – three countries where Beckett lived and worked – built biopolitical regimes and used censorship to shape cultural attitudes in support of their normalising engines. Intensified fears about population decline combined with anxiety about the fortitude of national character to foster new legislation regulating culture, alongside sex and reproduction, by variously outlawing abortion and artificial birth control, encouraging marriage and parenthood, discouraging divorce, banning pornography, and so forth (Brooke 2011; Ferriter 2009: 191–3; Hug 1999: 11–30, 143–60; Pavard 2019; Phillips 1999; Sigel 2002, 2011, 2013; Tagg 1993: 103–16). Fears that obscenity would corrupt the national body led governments to censor 'unnatural vice' and funnel sexual energies into the 'proper' channels (Heath 2010: 35–46; Hug 1999: 79–84; Huss 1990: 39–44). The biopolitical impulse that propelled such normalising projects also reinforced a commitment to domesticity. Seeking to shake off the nightmare of occupation, post-war France obsessed over personal, cultural and social hygiene and domesticity, reordering life around the normative family (Ross 1995: 1–11). As the French Empire crumbled, political economy shifted to the metropolis to regulate and discipline domestic space in a 'colonization of everyday life' (Ross 1995: 77–8). In Britain, middle-class respectability had long been associated with normative sexual standards. Stephen Brooke (2006) argues that the post-war period saw the working class take on a similar domesticity. Ireland, too, experienced industrial modernisation in the late 1950s and 1960s, seeing major surges in consumer culture around items like cars, fridges, washing machines and televisions that helped to make domesticity a 'new luxury' for many Irish, strengthening the nuclear family in the process (Daly 2016: 131–6, 370). Such socio-economic practices propped up the family with all its claims to normalcy and success.

Performing domesticity in the desolate surroundings of *Happy Days* ought to lay bare the absurdity of Winnie's commitments, but audience projection makes them seem credible. Watching Winnie 'cope', spectators become complicit in the production of her delusions of coping. Hence the tenacity of the stoic reading: the redemptive perversion. British pluck has tended to see itself embodied in

Winnie's tenacity, but only because the audience, too, is invested in coping. Projection, here, is central to Beckett's project for the theatre: we project heroism onto Winnie's futility rather than reflect on our own entanglement in ritualised consumerism. In one such scene, Winnie goes through the motions of preparing for the day by taking some medicine for her pain, applying her lipstick and putting on her hat, all while Willie begins his own routine, reading titbits from the newspaper to his wife (HD 15–19). Throughout this sequence, Willie's interjections and the memories they prompt in Winnie interrupt her gesture of putting on a hat. Unlike the reminder of her age and deterioration that stopped her from laying down the toothbrush, here the interruptions that stop her from putting on her hat work to extend her domestic temporality by giving her the excuse to delay the completion of her preparations for the day, filling up more time. The memories she shares do not contradict her commitment to changelessness, but help her perform domesticity with Willie. Winnie's activities are very much a labour of keeping up appearances to put her worries at bay – but there is nothing but failure here. Action itself (however put-upon) holds the affect of straight temporality in place while time nevertheless keeps moving forward.

In the second act, with Winnie buried now to her neck, the bell becomes the overdetermined reminder of her insecure position and the temporal gap between her and her audience. Beckett wanted the bell to be brutal and cutting for his production, like a knife striking metal (Beckett 1985: 141). The difference between the bell and the *défaillances* as the medium for disrupting temporal identification is that the bell is external, a more obviously oppressive force. In act two, with fewer options, Winnie usually tries to fall asleep only to be jolted awake by the bell. Inevitably, she turns again to whatever is available to her to speak about: Willie, her environment, her thoughts, the gun and bag (the only objects she can see), her body, or her stories. The *défaillances* slowly tear the audience from their temporal identification with Winnie. The bell expedites the process, slicing through that connection by interrupting Winnie's intentions and prompting Winnie to begin again. The jolt of the bell actualises the temporal rupture, and the audience can only escape the long duration it demands of Winnie if she distracts herself and thereby distracts them.

The final moments of the play bring an evening of regulated affects of success and failure to a head by leaving the audience in ambiguity. Willie appears on the front side of the mound with her, and he tries to crawl towards her but struggles before reaching towards his wife – or the gun, just off to her side – as he mutters her name, 'Win' (Beckett 1985: 134; HD 66–9). As in the first act, for Winnie his acknowledgement of her signals that this is another happy day, and so she rushes to bring it to a close by singing her end-of-the-day song, a brief love lyric from Franz Lehár's operetta *The Merry Widow* (1905). She closes her eyes to end the day, but the bell rings after she does so, forcing her to stay awake. Winnie has failed one last time. Her smile evaporates, and she and her husband look at each other as the play ends (HD 70). With the day not yet over according to the bell, Winnie has, by her own admission, exhausted her options. Only, perhaps, in turning to Willie is there a possibility for her to keep going. But, Willie is not bound to the earth or bell as his wife is – domestic time is seemingly gendered. Unlike Winnie, Willie has a range of options: he could abandon her, kill her, join her, or do nothing at all. The ending captures Winnie in the open, queer time she has spent the play avoiding, and the audience, too, sits in anticipation of relief and closure that will never come – but at least they get to leave the theatre and escape from Beckett's entrapment, if not from the mechanisms of regulation he exposes.

The last bell marks the audience's final separation from their temporal identification with Winnie and, unmoored as they are without leads from the character who has been their affective guide in this nearly vacant world they've endured, the spectators can't know if Winnie will find a way to busy herself once more. After so many iterations of the same affective pattern, is anything else imaginable? Ending the play in ambiguity, in their own affective queer time, leaves the audience in the most potent critical space available to them to consider what has transpired and how they have engaged with it (or not). If there are ways forward that don't partake in the sanctioned violence of the theatrical gaze, that might help to imagine a more progressive world, Beckett doesn't provide them. They are a projection of the audience. Instead, Beckett instrumentalises the performance–audience relationship into an aesthetic model of politics that enacts the process of subjection, and uses theatre's temporal affects to sway audiences into cheering for a woman to waste away into oblivion precisely because it makes them feel better about their own complicity. Beckett rejects failure as success. He rejects queerness as redemptive. He rejects theatre as liberating. Beckett's theatre regulates responses and acts like a normalising engine that builds and demarcates the range of affective, emotional and even intellectual possibilities – and it does so that we might, against the odds, come to see the part we play in making and perpetuating unhappy days.

Chapter 8

Beckett's Safe Words: Normalising Torture in *How It Is*

Dominic Walker

Do not get silly ideas into yr head about hurting. It is I the hurter of the two.
– Samuel Beckett, letter to Pamela Mitchel, 14 August 1954
(LII 492)

The most scandalous part of a scandal is getting used to it.
– Simone de Beauvoir, 'For Djamila Boupacha', *Le Monde*, 3 June 1960
(de Beauvoir and Halimi 1962: 220)

This essay is about how Samuel Beckett reacted to a perceived discursive normalisation of State violence during the War of Algerian Independence. Building on Emilie Morin's recent work (2017: 184–238), it will respond to Gisèle Halimi's observation that, by the late 1950s, an 'automatic routine' of rhetorical 'indignation' and signatory 'protests' had unintentionally helped to desensitise the French public to persistent State-sanctioned torture of Algerian citizens (de Beauvoir and Halimi 1962: 19). Andrew Gibson has noticed that Beckett's post-war work 'obstinately refuses [. . .] to get up to speed' with the kind of official rhetoric that drowned out the 'historical catastrophe' of French collaboration with a 'glib language of recovery' (2010a: 15–16). Beckett had to contend with a very different discursive situation in the late 1950s. The Algerian Revolution was an open, ongoing catastrophe with virtually universal public exposure (Shepard 2006: 66–8). While the 'vaguen[ed]' external referents of *Waiting for Godot* (1953) and *Three Novels* (1959) sometimes excruciatingly mimic the repression of historical memory in post-Vichy France (Pountney 1988: 149), Beckett would not have been able to put his work at the same challenging remove from history in an economy of language saturated with explicit political material. He responded by placing a deictic marker smack in the middle of *How*

It Is (1961), naming the narrator's lover-victim 'Pim' and, on three suggestively homophonic occasions, 'Pam', after the notorious legal acronym for prisoners approved for torture (PAM or *'pris les armes à la main'* ['captured with weapons']) (Beckett 2001: 87, 96, 99; hereafter HII; Branche 2007: 514–15). What's more, in a startling conflation of personal and political material, the narrator's 'wife above' happens to share a Christian name with Beckett's ex-lover, Pamela Mitchell, about whom he felt he was 'the hurter of the two' (HII 97; LII 492). This essay will suggest that the inclusion of the PAM referent is a provocation that points to the same spent language that was incapable of sustaining effective opposition to the Algerian War. Its incendiary confusion of love and torture is the violent product of a discursive environment in which words had become safe and violence had become normalised.

To start with, I am going to give a brief overview of the relevant context about torture during the Algerian War and its representations in the French press. Then I am going to detail two recent critical interpretations of the torture theme in *How It Is*, sandwiched around a reading from part two of Beckett's text. In the first of these interpretations, Adam Piette argues that *How It Is* 'materialises' a 'dialectic of victim and perpetrator' which 'raises questions about the continuity between French Resistance victimhood [...] and fascist-colonial violence' in Algeria (2016: 152). Piette reads the text through Jean-Paul Sartre's 'Colonialism Is a System' (1956), a half-historical, half-philosophical treatise on torture which he regards as the discursive 'trigger' for Beckett in 1958 (158). In the second interpretation, David Lloyd argues that *How It Is* can be understood in terms of Kant's ethical formalism and the 'system of representation' on which it depends (2010: 212). While the torturer's indifference to the suffering individual is preserved as form in a 'logic of substitution', Lloyd finds no evidence to indicate that Beckett's text is referring to French torturers in particular; it may not even refer to the physical act of torture at all (212). I will argue the following: that a critical misperception of *How It Is* as a straightforward continuation of Beckett's earlier pseudo-formalism means that Lloyd has overlooked at least one explicit historical referent concerning the Algerian Revolution; and that that referent cannot be the emphatically and exclusively male victims in Sartre's tendentiously philosophical account. Drawing on recent scholarship challenging androcentric histories of torture in Algeria, I will suggest that Beckett's provocative transposition of political and personal material is, at best, a parody of the 'logic of substitution' that the text 'waver[ingly]' condemns as the basis of real political torture (HII 173). At worst, *How It Is* might reciprocally normalise political sexual violence and normative romantic sadism, putting them on the same seemingly inescapable continuum of patriarchal cruelty, and perhaps even making them appear morally equivalent.

Predating the formation of the Front de libération nationale (FLN) by three years, Claude Bourdet's 1951 article for *L'Observateur*, 'Is there an Algerian Gestapo?', is the earliest published account of French State torture in Algeria (Shepard 2006: 66). Another article by Bourdet, who had himself been tortured by the Gestapo, appeared the same week in January 1955 as François Mauriac's 'The Question'; this was four months after the then 500-strong FLN launched their first attacks on targets across Algeria, and two months before the Governor General of Algeria, Jacques Soustelle, received his first official report about torture from the French military (Shepard 2006: 69–70). *Le Monde*, the centre-right daily newspaper founded at the behest of Charles de Gaulle, published an April 1956 opinion piece about torture in Algeria that invoked Nazi concentration camps, bringing the news to a mainstream audience for the first time. In February 1957, the leftish Catholic weekly newspaper *Témoignage Chrétien* printed a collection of letters by an army reservist stationed in Algeria, the first of a handful of accounts to be published by Christian organisations that year. Jean-Paul Sartre was moved by one such collection, *Des Rappelés Témoignent* (1957), to write an admiring article in the May 1957 edition of *Les Temps Modernes*, with the title 'You're Wonderful' (Shepard 2006: 66). This was one of three pieces on torture Sartre penned between April 1956 and 1958, along with 'Colonialism Is a System', published in *Les Temps Modernes* in March 1956, and 'A Victory', published in *L'Express* in April 1958 and reissued as the preface of Henri Alleg's *La Question* (1958). *La Question* itself was the first of seven first-person accounts of torture published by Beckett's friend and publisher Jérôme Lindon over the next four years, all of which were banned by the French government (Le Sueur 2005: 178–9).

Piette addresses two of Sartre's contributions. The first is 'Colonialism Is a System', which argues that the post-war renaissance of the discourse of rights was a liberal reaction to fascism that could not be sustained in peacetime in a colonial power. 'One of the functions of racism', Sartre writes, 'is to compensate the latent universalism of bourgeois liberalism: since all human beings have the same rights, the Algerian will be made a subhuman' (2001a: 45). France's overstretched 'universalism' snapped back into place as soon as an otherable group declined to cooperate with its geopolitical aims, leading to the exclusion of Algerian citizens from the category of the human. '[S]ince the natives are subhuman', Azzedine Haddour paraphrases, 'the Declaration of the Human Rights does not apply to them' (2001: 2).

Piette sees Sartre's preface to *La Question* as a more 'phenomenolog[ical]' counterpart to 'Colonialism Is a System' (2016: 158). Responding to Alleg's account of torture, Sartre begins by musing on the historical parallels between Nazi violence in France and French violence in Algeria. '[I]f fifteen years are enough to turn the victims into torturers', he declares, it is because 'anyone, at any time, [could] become a victim or a perpetrator' (Sartre 2001b: 73). For Sartre, the readiness with which this reversal can and did take place means that 'victim and perpetrator are one and the same image', an 'inseparable couple' in which the victim role is 'no more than a manifestation' of the role of the perpetrator (2001b: 66, 76). In fact, it is the victim 'who is really strong', who 'frighten[s]' the torturer by bringing him face-to-face with his inhumanity (2001a: 38). Piette argues that *How It Is* 'materialises' this 'dialectic' through its torture-couples, which 'stage the inseparability of torturer and tortured' and 'mimic the inversion of victim and torturer' in Sartre's essay (2016: 152, 166). Sartre's influence is particularly legible, Piette suggests, 'in the phenomenology of the interaction between the narrator and Pim' (158). For example, something like a handshake accidentally occurs at one point during their struggle, and with it a sudden apprehension, dimly perceived through 'the command and control structure of the torturing', of a 'more humane forum [. . .] based on species recognition and acknowledgement' (169). The handshake constitutes a 'role-reversal' on Sartre's model, since the narrator loses his 'species rights' in the act of depriving Pim of his legal ones (169). Just like Sartre's victim, it is Pim who has his humanity affirmed, who proves he 'belong[s] to the human species', precisely because of the torturer's determination to exclude him (Sartre 2001b: 74).

Historian Judith Surkis notes that many prominent discursive interventions in the torture crisis were characterised by 'macho bravado' (2010: 45). Sartre is singled out for his preface to *La Question*, which Surkis regards as a tendentious philosophical misappropriation of the facts, framing 'torture as a heroic trial of masculinity' to the exclusion of numerous women who underwent the same or similar ordeals (45–6). We have already seen that, for Sartre, the torture victim's experience is a dialectical event, a triumphant role-reversal that confirms his strength and humanity at the expense of the torturer. But Sartre seems to regard that struggle in exclusively masculine terms:

> This heroic masculinity thus stands in opposition to the diminished masculinity of his torturers, who Sartre describes as 'these little cads, proud of their strength, their youth, their number'. By contrast, wrote Sartre, 'Alleg is the really tough one, the only one who is really strong'. (Surkis 2010: 41)

It could be argued that Sartre is writing specifically about a man being tortured; but such tenaciously gendered rhetoric could, at the very least, be mistaken for an unrepresentative generalisation of the experience of all survivors of torture. If torture is the struggle to be recognised as human, that appears to mean the struggle to be recognised as man: 'it is for the title of *man* that the torturer pits himself against the tortured, and the whole thing happens as if they could not both belong to the human species' (Sartre 2001b: 74). '[W]hen it is the victim who wins', Sartre concludes, then it is 'farewell to supremacy and to *droit du seigneur*', the historic right of feudal landlords to have sex with whomever they pleased (77). In Sartre's histrionically Hegelian account, the master has been forced to recognise the slave, and what is being recognised is his 'virility' (Surkis 2010: 41).

French journalism, meanwhile, could hardly be accused of androcentric bias in its coverage of torture (Nashat and Tucker 1998: 111). Tortured women attracted far more media attention than their male counterparts, something that Christine Quinan attributes to prurience and racism (2014: 117). The two most notorious cases occurred three years apart, though there is shockingly little else to distinguish them. Djamila Bouhired was arrested on 9 April 1957 after planting a bomb in a milk bar in Algiers in September 1956. She was tortured for seventeen days and sentenced to death in July 1957, eventually provoking an international outcry; the British Labour Party and Bertrand Russell were among those to call for amnesty (Mikaberidze 2013: 72). *For Djamila Bouhired* (1957), a book published by Lindon's Éditions de Minuit and co-written by Georges Arnaud and Bouhired's lawyer, Jacques Vergès, graphically detailed the torture she underwent, which included having 'electrodes [placed] in her vagina and on her nipples' (Vince 2015: 84). The dramatic events of her court hearing, dubbed the 'Bomb Trial' by a titillated media, were headline news for a full month in 1957 (Cixous 2003). Bouhired became such a celebrity that she had a film made about her in 1958, *Jamila, the Algerian*; she is also a central figure in *The Battle of Algiers* (1966). Such notoriety clearly rattled the French establishment. Rumours were circulated that she had fallen in love with her torturer, a tactic used to discredit at least two other FLN prisoners; Jean Lartéguy, a former paratrooper, wrote a novel fictionalising the supposed affair, *The Centurions* (1960), which won an award at the Académie française (Rejali 2009: 490; 2007: 152). Beckett could not have been unaware of such rumours when he reproduced the lover-torturer trope in *How It Is*. Bouhired's name was 'a household word', as one historian puts it, 'for anyone concerned with the Algerian revolution', which Beckett certainly was (Gordon 1968: 54). He had his '[e]ars glued' to the radio throughout the siege of Algiers, for instance, according to a February 1960 letter to Barbara Bray (LIV 290).

Beckett is likely to have been apprised directly, then, of the arrest of Djamila Boupacha on 10 February 1960. Boupacha's ordeal was practically identical to that of Bouhired's. Following her arrest, Boupacha was tortured for thirty-three days and sentenced to death on 15 March after she admitted to planting an unexploded bomb in a café near the University of Algiers (Brown 2018: 83). Appalled by the lack of public reaction, Simone de Beauvoir took on Boupacha's cause, describing her torture in a controversially explicit article published in *Le Monde* on 3 June 1961 titled 'For Djamila Boupacha' in a deliberately weary echo of *For Djamila Bouhired*. De Beauvoir succeeded in 'provok[ing] a scandal in French and international opinion', something no recent journalism had been able to achieve (Vince 2015: 84). The article describes how Boupacha had been tortured with electric shocks; cigarette burns; a form of waterboarding known as '*la baignoire*' ('the bath'); being forced to drink foul water; having water pumped into her anus; rape with intermediate objects including a toothbrush and a beer bottle; and a series of stress positions nicknamed '*la corde*' ['the rope']. Rope is repeatedly mentioned among the narrator's small inventory in *How It Is* (Le Sueur 2001: 169; HII 8, 48, 54, 58, 150). According to Raphaëlle Branche, Boupacha's testimony reflects the experience of many survivors. 'Violent penetration, often using a piece of wood, a bottle etc., was frequent' for women prisoners; and, while men were also sexually assaulted in detention, 'abused men seldom describe[d] their sexual humiliation', so there were few, if any, contemporary reports (Branche 2009: 250; Lazreg 2008: 124–5). The notoriety of Bouhired and Boupacha, meanwhile, is consistent with the fact that 'The most publicised combatants of the FLN were women' (Nashat and Tucker 1998: 111).

Two prominent critics evoke reports of sexual torture against women in their reviews of *Comment c'est*. Writing in *Mercure de France* a fortnight after Beauvoir's *Le Monde* article, Jean-Jacques Mayoux interprets the narrator's attack as a sexual assault 'in Pim's arse' (rather than painstakingly avoiding 'the hole') with a non-specific 'tool of torture [*torture*]' (Mayoux 1979: 233; HII 85). He could well have Boupacha's account specifically in mind. Maurice Nadeau's review, published on 26 January 1961 in *L'Express*, describes *Comment c'est* as a story about a 'torturer who forms an amorous couple with his victim', an interpretation that is consistent with propaganda about Bouhired and other prisoners falling in love with their torturers (1979: 227). Nadeau even stresses the possibility of external referents in the text, asking, 'Are we in the realm of literature? Are we outside of it?', implying that it may not just be a literary fiction (228). It does not appear to be:

- drive it into the arse not the hole not such a fool the cheek a cheek (HII 85)
- when stabbed in the arse instead of crying he sings his song what a cunt this Pim (HII 85)
- or feel merely slow and the day comes we come to the day when stabbed in the arse now an open wound instead of the cry a brief murmur done it at last (HII 87)
- 2 speak blade in arse [. . .] 5 softer index in anus (HII 89)
- stab him simply in the arse that is so to speak and he will say anything what he can whereas proof I need proof so stab him in a certain way signifying answer once and for all (HII 91)
- the threat the bleeding arse the cracking nerves you invent but real (HII 93)

Why would it be 'fool[ish]', in the first quotation, to drive the opener into 'the hole' rather than 'the cheek'? I do not think that this is a facetious gag about a narrator comfortable with torture but squeamish about excrement. The historical explanation would be that, while gouging out someone's flesh was demonstrably torture, rape with an intermediate object might fail to meet the burden of proof. One of the legal ruses employed by the French government to circumvent Article 3 of the European Convention of Human Rights (ECHR) meant ensuring that the victim's body did not bear any visible wounds (Ross 1995: 118). This was why rape was used by the French military in Algeria. General Jacques Massu later described rape as 'functional torture', comparing it to 'the medical interventions of a surgeon or a dentist' (Ross 1995: 118). The narrator's litigious pedantry about avoiding 'the hole', in a context of organised violence, parallels the disturbing pedantry of French Army policy. Like General Massu, Beckett's narrator thinks he is cleverly circumventing the legal definition of a graver crime.

The preferred crime in this instance does, however, do external bodily damage. By avoiding 'the hole', the narrator inverts and confuses the spurious legal distinction between rape and torture that the French perpetrators exploited to do both. As the torture scene proceeds, that distinction is made to appear even more senseless. In the second quotation, Pim is a 'cunt' for being stabbed in the 'arse'. This is a gendered word that points towards a gendered context. The narrator's half-hearted transposition of women and men has reverted to the original; like Molloy, slits and rectums are '[a] matter of complete indifference to [him]' (Beckett 1979: 53). The reversion points out the feebleness of its own equivocation, at the same time likening that equivocation to the juridical alibi invoked by the authorities to insist that they were, not, in fact, engaged in torture. By the third quotation, the 'arse [. . .] cheek' has become an 'open wound', a new 'hole' that 'at last' makes the careful legalistic avoidance of penetration redundant. In the fourth quotation, 'finger in anus', it turns out the torturer's repertoire includes digital rape regardless, with 'softer' ridiculing the distinction in the first place, making the scene reappear in the merely 'amorous' light of Nadeau's review. In the fifth quotation, the narrator's technique for stabbing Pim in the arse has been altered in a 'certain way' – a final, definitive way ('once and for all') – that, again, seems to suggest no further pretence of a distinction between legally ambiguous sexual assault and verifiable torture. In the final quotation, the distinction between internal and external trauma has been confounded altogether; the site of injury is lawfully irrelevant should visible 'bleeding' occur, so the State's workaround has been a pointless exercise all along. The narrator is uncannily right to describe the scene as 'invent[ed]' but 'real'. While there is no evidence that Beckett amended his text to reflect Boupacha's account – '*Fin 6.6.60*', his sixth and final notebook reads, with knowing hellishness, just three days after Beauvoir's article – her ordeal was 'not exceptional' (P 477). Beckett likely encountered similar accounts elsewhere (Surkis 2010: 41). The method and outcome of her and Pim's tortures are virtually identical, with Boupacha left in 'a pool of her own blood' after she was ultimately raped with a beer bottle (de Beauvoir and Halimi 1962: 43–4). The only real difference is metonymic: Pim has been raped with an 'opener' instead of a thing to be opened (HII 41).

Boupacha's case was unusual only in that, unlike many 'other newspaper accounts of anonymous tortured women [that] were circulating', she actively wanted the details of her assault to be disseminated as widely as possible (Quinan 2014: 120). After seven years of conflict and crisis, public resistance to torture was at a disturbingly low ebb, and Boupacha hoped to shock the French public into caring again (Surkis 2010: 41). Her lawyer, Gisèle Halimi, describes their mutual frustration in *Djamila Boupacha* (1962), co-authored by De Beauvoir:

> The words were the same stale clichés: ever since torture had been used in Algeria there had always been the same words, the same expressions of indignation, the same, the same signatures to public protests, the same promises. This automatic routine had not abolished one set of electrodes or water-hoses; nor had it in any remotely effective way curbed the power of those who used them. (De Beauvoir and Halimi 1962: 19)

For Halimi, activist literature had been ineffective because of its docile, often self-regarding conformity to a rhetoric of 'indignation' that was practically official. What this looked like was the 'same[ness]' of 'words': an unthinking repetitiousness that is re-enacted by her text through its 'automatic' repetition of that very word, the 'same'. The list of forms of verbal protest, 'words', expressions', 'signatures', 'promises', are formed into a diminuendo, hushed up on the sibilance of 'promises' ['*promesses*'], the only word that points towards action. We are made to feel the 'remote[ness]' of these words from any praxis by their contrast with the stark materiality of the two objects of torture, picked at random and unanswerably strewn about in a sentence that nearly equates the 'automatic routine' of dissent with the repetitive procedures of torture itself. The 'same[ness]' of language, diminishing returns of meaning on a given form as it loses its symbolic power, is linked directly to the 'power' of the torturers. In Halimi's dialectical view, French paratroopers were allowed to continue to brutalise their victims with impunity partly because of this congenial discursive environment. She was far from alone in thinking so.

The normalisation of torture, then, depended in part on the 'same[ness]' and 'routine' of anti-war literature. The more reports and polemics that appeared, the more each scandal became interchangeable with the others. The logic, here, is one of substitution: every torture victim becomes alike. As David Lloyd sees it, this is the precondition of torture as such. In the final chapter of *Irish Culture and Colonial Modernity*, he explores how that 'logic of substitution' is made to appear in *How It Is* (2010: 212). The text's 'principle of intersecting seriality' shows that the liberal principle of formal equality before the law is a hair's-breadth away from becoming the torturer's indifference to the suffering individual ('what the fuck [. . .] does it matter who suffers') (Lloyd 2010: 212; HII 176). Immanuel Kant's *Critique of Practical Reason* (1788) provides the model of a 'split subject' in *How It Is*, half 'subject of reason' and half 'pathological subject' (Lloyd 2010: 216). The pathological subject is the 'subject that undergoes' contingent things like 'needing, desiring, enjoying and suffering' (216). It is the object of unavailable 'laws of natural causality', and this makes it an opaque 'object to itself', too (209). For this reason, the pathological subject is unfree to produce universally applicable maxims, since it is ruled by laws amongst which it cannot reliably orientate itself. This is why the 'subject of reason' has to be a 'subject without properties': its maxims cannot 'rise to the level of a moral law for all' unless it has been purged of all circumstance and particularity (209).

The 'moment of universality' that Kant finds once his subject has had all its properties deleted is the basis of the '"deep structure" of historical conditions' underpinning torture in the modern 'security state' (218). For Lloyd, Kant's moral law is like legal equality because they both answer to the 'need to predicate on the multitude of contingent individuals a single and universal form for the moral law, without which ethics would be mired in the particularities of singular pleasures and pains' (211). This is possible only if those particularities are 'abstracted from', leaving a merely 'formal law' intact that can be applied to all subjects as if they were 'alike'. This 'as if' is a 'metaphor' because it suspends differences to bring 'disparate subjects' together (212). Like a metaphor, it works centrifugally to attract samenesses to the centre; it is premised on the potential equivalence of things ('this is that') – or as Lloyd puts it, a logic of substitution. The logic of substitution means that Kant's ethics and the rule of law are both based on a 'system of representation' in which a 'single figure' is made to 'stand for' everyone, in that aspect of themselves that is taken for 'universality', so that they can be subject to universal law (212).

Lloyd's argument is that Beckett's series of replaceable torturer/victims in *How It Is* demonstrates the internal logic of that system of representation (211). Representation, he maintains, is an idealist shortcut that makes all subjects 'alike' in order, ostensibly, to ensure legal equality (212). But this hellish regime of fungibility is not necessarily as bad as it sounds, because the text:

refuses to depart from the 'pathological' world of the feeling subject who appears as an object for himself and an object for others whom he takes as his objects in an endless series of substitutions, 'tormentor always of the same and victim always of the same'. In this respect, it registers the conditions of a world in which the determination that every subject is an end in himself and not a means for others is systematically traduced. (Lloyd 2010: 211)

How It Is is not a symptom but a 'dark parody of the *Second Critique*', because it uses torture figuratively to imagine the conditions of possibility for a world in which subjects constitute means for one another rather than ends (211). The figuratively tortured subject represents that new world because it is the opposite of the 'dominant ethical paradigm' that has us believe that there can be no equality of justice without Kant's subject of reason, the sovereign subject whose disinterestedness ends up being like a torturer's indifference (211). For Lloyd, then, it is not as troubling as it might be to think of being tortured as a utopian sublime of generosity, because '*How It Is* is not a representation of the world as it appears to be, but a demonstration of its inner logic' (211). Unlike Kantian ethics or the laws we live under, Beckett's text does not exclude the 'pathological' content that determines each subject 'in its particularity'. Being about the most extreme and impermissible things that a human can do or undergo, the most particular pains and pleasures they can enjoy or suffer, *How It Is* is exclusively about the pathological subject. As a result, Beckett's text is able to block the symbolic move that would otherwise isolate the universal element in all subjects in order to make them formally alike. There can be no 'ascent from particularity to representation', no 'metaphorical sublimation' of difference in a 'single figure' (211). The text can't represent anything in particular, because it is representing particularity as such.

For Lloyd, this stops *How It Is* from being egregious thematisation of real historical suffering and even allows torture to become a qualifiedly utopian image. It is about a more generous form of relationality, a 'life in common' founded on what is really universal: 'the commonality of the needing, desiring, enjoying and suffering human life that the split subject and its complementary couple, torturer-tortured, subject-object, have subordinated under the category of the "pathological"' (HII 77; Lloyd 2010: 216). The text's violence, shockingly paralleled by the historical fact of torture in Algeria (but crucially not representing it), helps to check irresponsibly utopian readings by providing an approximation of the resistance any such imaginary transformation of social relations would and does encounter in the real world (one of the readiest objections being: if there was no universal law, how would you stop people from torturing each other?). But this ethical failsafe requires a delicate balance. If the text tips too far towards utopianism, it would entail a horrifically exploitative use of real historical suffering for dreamy political ends. If the text tips too far away from utopianism, it would exploit the same suffering for indifferently aesthetic ends. To get the balance right, the distance from the real referent of torture needed to be calculated exactly, much as Beckett calculated the distance of *Endgame* (1956) from nuclear warfare in Theodor Adorno's reading of the play (2013: 339). As Lloyd understands it, Beckett's earlier pseudo-formalism has been used, again, to put *How It Is* at the most productively ambiguous remove from its historical event, refusing to sugar-coat the horror or to let us off the hook, yet still leaving a grain of hope intact for those who want to find it, the only ethical quantity and a representative one at that.

In his essay on *How It Is*, Piette describes how a *de facto* 'colonial clause' allowed the French government to contravene the stipulation in Article 3 of the European Convention on Human Rights (ECHR) that 'No one shall be subjected to torture or to inhuman or degrading treatment or punishment' (Piette 2016: 152). The clause Piette identifies is Article 63. It permits '[a]ny state' to declare 'that the present Convention shall extend to all or any of the territories for whose international relations it is responsible', implying that the Convention does not already extend to this euphemism for occupied countries (European Court of Human Rights 1994: 30). While the British government used this defence to torture people in Northern Ireland and Cyprus, there was never any need for the French authorities to resort to this workaround in Algeria. They instead relied on the vanishingly significant distinction between prisoners of war, or 'POW', and what they called '*pris les armes à la main*' ('captured with weapons'), or PAM (Branche 2007: 550). This legal debacle was widely publicised, with the phrase '*pris les armes à la main*' appearing in no fewer than forty-five separate articles in *Le Monde* during the war. The International Committee of the Red Cross, which inspected 'detention centres' in Algeria in November 1956 and July 1957, pressed the French government to recognise enemy combatants as POWs rather than PAMs, which would have protected them under Article 3 of the ECHR (Branche 2007: 546). But on 13 March 1958, General Raoul Salan confirmed French policy in a memorandum to the army, writing that 'It is well settled that the detained must not be considered prisoners of war. The Geneva Conventions are not applicable to them' (Draper 2013: 596).

Ruby Cohn points out that the name 'Pim', which was the working title of *How It Is* from the first notebook, 'puns in French on *pain* or bread, the so-called staff of life', because the 'i' would be pronounced in French as an 'a' (Cohn 2004: 257). The names 'Pam' and 'Pam Prim' appear on four occasions in the text (HII, 111, 97, 98, 99), all pertaining to a relationship the narrator has had in his 'life above' (HII 93). Despite the homophone, Cohn thinks of Pim and 'Pam Prim' as distinct characters, which they might be, though if she is right then the meaning of the distinction must be that it is almost immaterial, such is the extent of their similarities (2004: 258). Krim and Kram are a parallel case, making it less convincing to attribute the slippage to indifferent wordplay (HII 111). It is surely not a coincidence that Krim Belkacem was the name of the only surviving member of the founders of the FLN and its *de facto* leader from 1959; he signed the Évian Accords on behalf of Algeria in March 1962 (Evans 2012: 248).) In the life below, Pim is assaulted in 'the arse' with an 'opener' to make him speak or scream or sing on the narrator's behalf before the relationship, such as it is, is abandoned (HII 85). In life above, which specifies the connection between Pim and Pam with another homophone ('wife above'), 'Pam Prim' has attempted suicide after a 'little scene' of hopeful anal eroticism or sadism fails to 'resuscitate' a relationship that has become sexually less interesting (HII 97, 93, 111). Both "Pams" have therefore been on the wrong end of determined attempts to form or salvage romantic relationships 'through the arse', with the difference that one has been sexually assaulted with a domestic object in a systematic way akin to political torture (HII 111).

As well as being a legal euphemism for people fit for torture, 'Pam' was, of course, a name with personal associations for Beckett. In 1953, he started a three-year-long, intermittent but 'intense [...] romantic and sexual relationship' with Pamela Mitchell, an agent for Harold Oram, which originally held the rights for *Waiting for Godot* in the United States (Knowlson 1996: 398–405). Something about Beckett's affair with Mitchell seems to have inspired the generalised tormentor–victim relationships in *How It Is*. On 14 August 1954, around a year into their relationship, Beckett gave Mitchell some advice that anticipates its dyadic structure precisely: 'Do not get silly ideas into yr head about hurting. It is I the hurter of the two' (LII 492). He was probably not wrong. Beckett 'brusquely' ended the relationship with Mitchell in September 1956, shortly after she proposed moving permanently to Paris (Knowlson 1996: 400). His rationalisations make uncomfortable reading. 'I don't want you to forget me', he insists on 28 September, 'but I think it would be the best thing for you. I'm over, as sure as if they were on their way to measure me for the box' (LII 658). Beckett began the first 'Pim' manuscript in the summer of 1958 (HII 199).

I want to suggest that the inclusion of this conspicuous historical referent unsettles Lloyd's formalist reading of *How It Is*. '*How It Is*', Lloyd claimed, 'is not a representation of the world as it appears to be, but a demonstration of its inner logic' (2010: 211). The historical fact of torture played a part in the text, insofar as it might sober up incontinent dreamers; but its distance from that circumstance had to be calculated exactly, otherwise it would constitute the very kind of representation Beckett was critiquing as the inner 'logic of substitution' that allows torture to happen in the first place. This would, in fact, almost certainly have been the pseudo-formalist aesthetic keen readers of Beckett expected from *How It Is*. It would also be characteristic of him to disappoint them. In my view, the Pim/Pam name throws off what would otherwise be a more traditionally Beckettian imbalance of dense inner logics and light referents, slamming the text into historical particularity in a surprising departure from Beckett's earlier historical reticence. Beckett has mapped a scene of romantic sadness from his own life 'above' onto State-sanctioned torture and, I am suggesting, the torture of FLN women in particular. It is hard to resist the conclusion that the real 'trigger' of *How It Is*, which was called 'Pim' from the beginning of its composition in summer 1958 right up to its publication in 1961, was the simple homonym of PAM, '*pris les armes à la main*', and Pam, Pamela Mitchell, about whom Beckett felt, like the narrator of the text, that he was 'the hurter of the two'. If this is true, *How It Is* not only does not refuse 'metaphorical sublimation and the ascent from particularity to representation' (Lloyd 2010: 212); in one horrifying respect it makes that ascent all too readily. Tortured revolutionary women are made to stand for Beckett's ex, and Beckett's ex is made to stand for tortured revolutionary women. And if that substitution is not provocative enough, this one incident of romantic disappointment or cruelty is made to stand for *all* romantic travails as the text pans out to 'billions of us', then all relationships characterised by a power imbalance: 'pedant dunce' etc. (HII 185), then all situations in which people hurt one other, presumably including torture. The pathological world of the feeling subject is not a world that refuses the ascent from particularity to representation, *pace* Lloyd. Its 'intersecting seriality' is not the gift of the refusal of metaphorical generalisations, a utopian moment where the 'total permutability' of cathexes get to dance their 'radiant measure', as Murphy might say (M 62). Its seriality is specifically a consequence of *not* refusing the metaphorical sublimation that would group all power imbalances together in the single figure of the tormentor and victim, leniently made reversible so that 'what the fuck [...] does it matter who suffers' can stop 'waver[ing]' and become a safely rhetorical question, as the text's absence of punctuation provocatively allows it to be (HII 173).

With this grammatical open-endedness in mind, I want to conclude that, through its provocative normalisation of torture, *How It Is* raises a series of unanswered normative questions. Is it possible to pan out from personal circumstances to political structures, because they are both manifestations of a single norm? If so, to what extent should we expect normal life to shape or be shaped by those structures? Are the same normative power dynamics at work in individual relationships at work in historical struggles? Is the narrator symbolically torturing Pim, and if so, what relationship does that symbol have to real historical torture? Is every degree of domination in normative personal relationships qualitatively the same thing as political domination? Does being casually patriarchal, for instance, participate in the same everyday power structures as organised sexual violence in the context of imperialism, as *How It Is* seems to suggest? Would that thought horrify or console people who are normally patriarchal? Does it let torturers off the hook by making their violence look as normal as hurting people emotionally, or does it make people like Beckett and Sartre more uncomfortably complicit with power all the way up? Could it, in a perverse sense, romanticise normal everyday social violence by making it a tragically universal characteristic of human life, with torture being a hyperbole rather than a symbol for it? Or does the text alert us to that possibility, in the context of the 'war with no name', by being both blatantly explicit with names and weirdly inexplicit with content, through a kind of symbolic overdetermination? Does the thin integument of safe words holding back real torture from its everyday simulacra really scare us, or is it only there to take the edge off through phantasmatic mastery, the mild narcosis of representation potentiated by its closeness to the real thing, like a theme park ride? Could *How It Is* be pointing to the innocuousness of representation, of safe words, to show us how remote they are from praxis, even when they have been supercharged with personal and historical meaning, as in PAM? Does the text suggest that words will always be too safe, irrespective of what happens in the economy of language, from Hemingway's parsimonious 'theory of omission' to the compulsive explicitation of libertarian freedom of speech activists, whom Beckett sometimes disconcertingly resembles? Does it tell us to be more conscientious word-users, to painstakingly discriminate between all forms of violence, so that the question of what is normal doesn't obtain? Is it positing a 'nominalist ethics' that demands we see all suffering as absolutely particular and ungroupable, a kind of hyper-intersectionality? Or does it make the point, as numerous critics have, that politics and history should be bracketed in Beckett's work, first because he is a staunchly apolitical writer, and later because history and politics really are qualitatively unlike personal and aesthetic experiences, apart from when they intersect? And if so, why write a text normalising torture at a time when torture was *the* headline political story, and remained so for years? Because torture had been normalised by the very texts that sought to denormalise torture? Or because Beckett really did think that torture was continuous with normal life? What is the thing being normalised, and what is the normal? Do state actors torture because domination is the rule of normal life, where they learn to want to hurt? Or is that life a kind of after-image of the possibility of torture, its sublime? What comes first in our imaginary? How *is* it?

Bibliography

Government statutes and legislation

Criminal Law Amendment Act 1935, *Irish Statute Book*, section 17, <http://www.irishstatutebook.ie/eli/1935/act/6/enacted/en/print.html> (last accessed 23 August 2019).
European Court of Human Rights (1994), *European Convention on Human Rights*, Strasbourg: Council of Europe.

Letters

Beckett, S. (2009), *The Letters of Samuel Beckett: Vol. I, 1929–1940*, ed. G. Craig, M. Fehsenfeld, D. Gunn and L. Overbeck, Cambridge: Cambridge University Press.
— (2011), *The Letters of Samuel Beckett: Vol. II, 1941–1956*, ed. G. Craig, M. Fehsenfeld, D. Gunn and L. Overbeck, Cambridge: Cambridge University Press.
— (2014), *The Letters of Samuel Beckett: Vol. III, 1957–1965*, ed. G. Craig, M. Fehsenfeld, D. Gunn and L. Overbeck, Cambridge: Cambridge University Press.
— (2016), *The Letters of Samuel Beckett: Volume IV, 1966–1989*, ed. G. Craig, M. Fehsenfeld, D. Gunn and L. Overbeck, Cambridge: Cambridge University Press.

Primary sources

The McGreevy Correspondence, MS10402, Trinity College, Dublin.
'Pim', Notebook 6, Samuel Beckett Collection, Harry Ransom Center, University of Texas at Austin.
The *Watt* Manuscripts, Samuel Beckett Collection, Harry Ransom Center, University of Texas at Austin.

Secondary sources

Ackerley, C. J. (2010), *Demented Particulars: The Annotated* Murphy, Edinburgh: Edinburgh University Press.

Ackerley, C. J. and S. E. Gontarski (eds) (2004), *The Grove Companion to Beckett*, New York: Grove Press.

Adorno, T. (2013), *Aesthetic Theory*, ed. G. Adorno and R. Tiedmann, trans. R. Hullot-Kentor, London: Bloomsbury.

Agamben, G. (1998), *Homo Sacer: Sovereign Power and Bare Life*, Stanford: Stanford University Press.

Alleg, H. (2006), *The Question*, trans. J. Calder, Lincoln, NE: University of Nebraska Press.

Anderton, J. (2016), *Beckett's Creatures: Art of Failure after the Holocaust*, London: Bloomsbury.

Bair, D. (1991), *Samuel Beckett: A Biography*, London: Vintage.

Balzac, H. (1951), *Old Goriot*, trans. M. Crawford, London: Penguin.

Baron-Cohen, S. (1995), *Mindblindness*, Cambridge, MA: MIT Press.

— (2003), *The Essential Difference*, New York: Basic Books.

Barry, E. (2005), 'Translating nationalism', *Irish Studies Review*, 13.4, pp. 505–15.

Barry, E., U. Maude and L. Salisbury (eds) (2016), *Beckett, Medicine and the Brain*, Special Issue of *Journal of Medical Humanities*, 37.2.

Barthes, R. (1977a), *Fragments d'un discours amoureux*, Paris: Éditions du Seuil.

— (1977b), *Roland Barthes by Roland Barthes*, trans. R. Howard, New York: Hill and Wang.

— (1977c), 'Introduction to the structural analysis of narratives', in *Music, Image, Texts*, trans. S. Heath, London: Fontana Press, pp. 79–124.

— (1978), *A Lover's Discourse: Fragments*, trans. R. Howard, New York: Hill and Wang.

Beckett, S. (1938), *Murphy*, New York: Grove Press.

— (1957), *Fin de Partie*, Paris: Les Éditions de Minuit.

— (1974), *Oh Les Beaux Jours suivi de Pas moi*, Paris: Les Éditions de Minuit.

— (1979), *The Beckett Trilogy*, London: Picador.

— (1983), *Disjecta: Miscellaneous Writings and a Dramatic Fragment*, ed. R. Cohn, London: Calder.

— (1985), *Happy Days: The Production Notebook of Samuel Beckett*, ed. J. Knowlson, London: Faber and Faber.

— (1992), *Dream of Fair to Middling Women*, ed. E. O'Brien and E. Fournier, Dublin: Black Cat.

— (1995), *Samuel Beckett: The Complete Short Prose*, ed. S. E. Gontarski, New York: Grove Press.

— (1999), *Proust and Three Dialogues with Georges Duthuit*, London: Calder.
— (2001), *How It Is: A Critical-Genetic Edition*, ed. E. O'Reilly, London: Routledge.
— (2006a), *The Complete Dramatic Works*, London: Faber and Faber.
— (2006b), 'Endgame', in *The Complete Dramatic Works*, London: Faber and Faber, pp. 89–134.
— (2006c), 'Waiting for Godot', in *The Complete Dramatic Works*, London: Faber and Faber, pp. 7–88.
— (2009a), *Endgame*, ed. R. MacDonald, London: Faber and Faber.
— (2009b), *Watt*, ed. C. Ackerley, London: Faber and Faber.
— (2010a), *Happy Days*, ed. J. Knowlson, London: Faber and Faber.
— (2010b), *The Unnamable*, ed. S. Connor, London: Faber and Faber.
— (2012), *Samuel Beckett: Collected Poems*, ed. S. Lawlor and J. Pilling, London: Faber and Faber.
— (2013), *Happy Days*, New York: Grove Press.
— (2015), *Echo's Bones*, ed. M. Nixon, London: Faber and Faber.
Bersani, L. (1990), *Culture of Redemption*, Cambridge, MA: Harvard University Press.
— (1995), *Homos*, Cambridge, MA: Harvard University Press.
Bhabha, H. (2004), *The Location of Culture*, London: Routledge.
Bialas W. and A. Rabinbach (eds) (2007), *Nazi Germany and the Humanities: How German Academics Embraced Nazism*, New York: Oneworld.
Bigelow, G. (2003), *Fiction, Famine and the Rise of Economics in Victorian Britain and Ireland*, Cambridge: Cambridge University Press.
Bixby, P. (2010), *Samuel Beckett and the Postcolonial Novel*, Cambridge: Cambridge University Press.
— (2018), '"this … this … thing": The Endgame Project, corporeal difference, and the ethics of witnessing', in P. Bixby and S. Kennedy (eds), *(Dis)embodied Beckett*, Special Issue of *Journal of Beckett Studies*, 27.1, pp. 112–27.
Blau, H. (2003), *Sails of the Herring Fleet: Essays on Beckett*, Ann Arbor: University of Michigan Press.
Bolin, J. (2013), *Beckett and the Modern Novel*, Cambridge: Cambridge University Press.
Bourdieu, P. (2000), *Pascalian Meditations*, Stanford: Stanford University Press.
Boxall, P. (2004), 'Beckett and homoeroticism', in L. Oppenheim (ed.), *Palgrave Advances in Samuel Beckett Studies*, New York: Palgrave Macmillan, pp. 110–32.
Branche, R. (2007), 'Torture of terrorists? Use of torture in a "war against terrorism": justifications, methods and effects: the case of France in Algeria, 1954–1962', *International Review of the Red Cross (IRRC)*, 89.867, pp. 543–60.

— (2009), 'Sexual violence in the Algerian War', in D. Herzog (ed.), *Brutality and Desire*, London: Routledge, pp. 247–60.
Brooke, S. (2006), 'Bodies, sexuality and the "modernization" of the British working classes, 1920s to 1960s', *International Labor and Working-Class History*, 69, pp. 104–22.
— (2011), *Sexual Politics: Sexuality, Family Planning, and the British Left from the 1880s to the Present Day*, Oxford: Oxford University Press.
Brown, H. (2018), 'From sensation to representation: the torture of Djamila Boupacha during the Algerian War', *Women in French Studies*, 26, pp. 83–95.
Byron, M. (ed.) (2007), *Samuel Beckett's* Endgame, Rodopi: Amsterdam.
Campbell, T. and R. Esposito (2006), 'Interview', *diacritics* 36.2, pp. 49–56.
Canny, N. (1983), 'Edmund Spenser and the development of an Anglo-Irish identity', *Yearbook of English Studies*, 13, pp. 1–19.
Carleton, W. (1852), *The Squanders of Squander Castle*, 2 vols, London: Office of the Illustrated London Library, <https://archive.org/details/squanderscastle00carlgoog> (last accessed 13 May 2020).
Carrard, P. (2001), 'History as a kind of writing: Michel de Certeau and the poetics of historiography', *The South Atlantic Quarterly*, 100.2, pp. 465–82.
Carville, C. (2018), *Samuel Beckett and the Visual Arts*, Cambridge: Cambridge University Press.
Catanzaro, M. (2007), 'Masking and the social construct of the body in Beckett's *Endgame*', in M. Byron (ed.), *Samuel Beckett's* Endgame, Amsterdam: Rodopi, pp. 165–88.
Cavell, S. (1998), *Must We Mean What We Say?* Cambridge: Cambridge University Press.
Chiang, M. (2018), *Beckett's Intuitive Spectator: Me to Play*, Basingstoke: Palgrave Macmillan.
Cixous, H. (2003), 'Letter to Zohra Drif', trans. E. Pronewitz, *College Literature*, 30.1, pp. 82–90.
Cohn, R. (1980), *Just Play: Beckett's Theatre*, Princeton: Princeton University Press.
— (2004), *A Beckett Canon*, Ann Arbor: University of Michigan Press.
Connor, S. (2008), 'The shakes: conditions of tremor', *The Senses and Society*, 3.1, pp. 205–20.
Corkery, D. (1931), *Synge and Anglo-Irish Literature*, Cork: Cork University Press.
Critchley, S. (2014), *Very Little ... Almost Nothing: Death, Philosophy, Literature*, London: Routledge.
Curtis, L. P. (1970), 'The Anglo-Irish predicament', *Twentieth Century Studies*, 4, pp. 37–63.
Daly, M. (2016), *Sixties Ireland: Reshaping the Economy, State and Society, 1957–1973*, Cambridge: Cambridge University Press.
Davidson, A. (2001), *The Emergence of Sexuality: Historical Epistemology*

and the Formation of Concepts, Cambridge, MA: Harvard University Press.

Davidson, M. (2007), '"Every man his specialty": Beckett, disability and dependence', *Journal of Literary Disability*, 1.2, pp. 55–68.

Davies, (2019), 'Crawling in the Flanders mud: Samuel Beckett, war writing, and scatological pacifism', *Journal of War and Culture Studies*, 13.2, pp. 145–62.

— (forthcoming), *Samuel Beckett and the Second World War*, London: Bloomsbury.

Dean, T. (2000), *Beyond Sexuality*, Chicago: Chicago University Press.

de Beauvoir, S. and G. Halimi (1962), *Djamila Boupacha: The Story of the Torture of a Young Algerian Girl which Shocked Liberal French Opinion*, trans. P. Green, New York: Macmillan.

de Certeau, M. (1993), *The Writing of History*, trans. T. Conley, New York: Columbia University Press.

de la Durantaye, L. (2016), *Beckett's Art of Mismaking*, Cambridge, MA: Harvard University Press.

Deleuze, G. (1995), *Difference and Repetition*, New York: Columbia University Press.

Derrida, J. (1968), 'From a restricted to a general economy', in *Writing and Difference*, Chicago: University of Chicago Press, pp. 251–77.

— (1997), *Of Grammatology*, trans. G. Spivak, Baltimore: Johns Hopkins University Press.

Deutsch, H. (2015), 'Deformity', in R. Adams, B. Reiss and D. Serlin (eds), *Keywords for Disability Studies*, New York: New York University Press, pp. 52–4.

Dickinson, D., R. Huxtable and M. Parker (2010), *The Cambridge Medical Ethics Workbook*, 2nd edn, Cambridge: Cambridge University Press.

Doane, M. (1991), *Femmes Fatales*, London: Routledge.

Dolan, J. (2005), *Utopia in Performance: Finding Hope at the Theatre*, Ann Arbor: University of Michigan Press.

Donnelly, J. (1995), 'Mass eviction and the Great Famine', in C. Póirtéir (ed.), *The Great Irish Famine: The Thomas Davis Lecture Series*, Dublin: Mercier Press, pp. 155–73.

Dowd, G. (2012), 'Beckettian pain, in the flesh: singularity, community and the work', in M. Tanaka, Y. Tajiri and M. Tsushima (eds), *Samuel Beckett and Pain*, New York: Rodopi, pp. 67–91.

Draper, K. (2013), 'Why a war without a name may need one: policy-based application of international humanitarian law in the Algerian War', *Texas International Law Journal*, 48.3, pp. 575–603.

Driver, T. (1961), 'Beckett by the Madeleine', in L. Graver and R. Federman (eds), *Samuel Beckett: The Critical Heritage*, London: Routledge and Kegan Paul, pp. 217–23.

Effinger, E. (2011), 'Beckett's posthuman: the ontopology of *The Unnamable*', *Samuel Beckett Today/Aujourd'hui*, 23, pp. 369–81.

Esposito, R. (2008), *Bíos: Biopolitics and Philosophy*, Minneapolis: University of Minnesota Press.
— (2012), *Third Person*, trans. Z. Hanafi, Cambridge: Polity Press.
Evans, B. (2013), 'How autism became autism', *History of Human Sciences*, 26.3, pp. 3–31.
Evans, M. (2012), *Algeria: France's Undeclared War*, Oxford: Oxford University Press.
Felman, S. (1992), 'Camus' *The Plague*, or a monument to witnessing', in S. Felman and D. Laub (eds), *Testimony: Crises of Witnessing in Literature, Psychoanalysis, and History*, New York: Routledge, pp. 93–119.
Fifield, P. (2009), 'Gaping mouths and bulging bodies: Beckett and Francis Bacon', *Journal of Beckett Studies*, 18.1–2, pp. 57–71.
Fillingim, R. (2017), 'Individual differences in pain: understanding the mosaic that makes pain personal', *Pain*, 158.4, Suppl. 1, pp. S11–S18.
Forti, S. (2006), 'The biopolitics of souls: racism, Nazism, and Plato', *Political Theory*, 34.1, pp 9–32.
Foucault, M. (1990), *The History of Sexuality: An Introduction, Volume 1*, New York: Random House.
— (1991), 'Governmentality', in G. Burchell, C. Gordon and P. Miller (eds), *The Foucault Effect: Studies in Governmentality*, Chicago: University of Chicago Press, pp. 87–104.
— (1997), *Ethics: The Essential Writings I*, ed. P. Rabinov, London: Penguin.
— (1998), *The Will to Knowledge: The History of Sexuality Volume One*, trans. R. Hurley, London: Penguin.
— (2003), *Society Must Be Defended: Lectures at the Collège de France, 1975–1976*, trans. D. Macey, London: Picador.
— (2008), *Psychiatric Power: Lectures at the Collège de France, 1973–1974*, trans. G. Burchell, New York: Picador.
— (2011), *The Courage of Truth*, trans. G. Burchell, Basingstoke: Palgrave Macmillan.
Freeman, E. (2010), *Time Binds: Queer Temporalities, Queer Histories*, Durham, NC: Duke University Press.
Freud, S. [1905] (1979), 'Three essays on the theory of sexuality', in *On Sexuality*, London: Pelican, pp. 31–169.
Frith, U. (2003), *Autism: Explaining the Enigma*, London: Blackwell.
Frith, U. and F. Happé (1999), 'Theory of mind and self-consciousness: what is it like to be autistic?', *Mind and Language*, 14.1, pp. 1–22.
Gallese, V. and A. Goldman (1998), 'Mirror neurons and the simulation theory of mind-reading', *Trends in Cognitive Science*, 2.12, pp. 493–501.
Gallese, V., L. Fadiga, L. Fogassi and G. Rizzolatti (1996), 'Action recognition in the premotor cortex', *Brain*, 119, pp. 593–609.
Garland-Thompson, R. (1997), *Extraordinary Bodies: Figuring Physical*

Disability in American Culture and Literature, New York: Columbia University Press.
Garner Jr., S. (1994), *Bodied Spaces: Phenomenology and Performance in Contemporary Drama*, Ithaca: Cornell University Press.
Garrison, A. (2009), 'Faintly struggling things: inscrutable life in Beckett's *The Unnamable*', in S. Kennedy and K. Weiss (eds), *Samuel Beckett: History, Memory, Archive*, New York: Palgrave Macmillan, pp. 89–111.
Gibson, A. (1996), *Towards a Postmodern Theory of Narrative*, Edinburgh: Edinburgh University Press.
— (2006), *Beckett and Badiou: The Pathos of Intermittency*, Oxford: Oxford University Press.
— (2010a), *Samuel Beckett*, London: Reaktion.
— (2010b), 'Beckett, de Gaulle and the Fourth Republic, 1944–49: *L'Innommable* and *En attendant Godot*', *Limit(e) Beckett 1*, pp. 1–26, <http://www.limitebeckett.paris-sorbonne.fr/one/gibson.html> (last accessed 27 August 2019).
— (2010c), 'Afterword: "the skull the skull the skull the skull in Connemara": Beckett, Ireland and elsewhere', in S. Kennedy (ed.), *Beckett and Ireland*, Cambridge: Cambridge University Press, pp. 179–203.
— (2015), 'Beckett, Vichy, Maurras, and the body: *Premier Amour* and *Nouvelles*', *Irish University Review*, 45.2, pp. 281–301.
Gierow, K. (2007), '1969 Nobel prize in literature presentation speech', trans. J. Garforth, in *Dictionary of Literary Biography, Vol. 329: Nobel Prize Laureates in Literature, Part I – Aganon–Eucken*, Detroit: Gale, pp. 87–8.
Gilbert, P. and J. Mascaro (2017), 'Compassion fears, blocks and resistances: an evolutionary investigation', in E. Seppälä, E. Simon-Thomas, S. Brown, M. Worline, C. Cameron and J. Doty (eds), *The Oxford Handbook of Compassion Science*, Oxford: Oxford University Press, pp. 399–418.
Gontarski, S. E. (2017), *Beckett's* Happy Days: *A Manuscript Study*, Columbus: Ohio State University Press.
Gooch, G. (1920), *Germany and the French Revolution*, London: Longmans, Green.
Gordon, D. (1968), *Women of Algeria: An Essay on Change*, Cambridge, MA: Harvard University Press.
Gordon, L. (1998), *The World of Samuel Beckett, 1906–1946*, New Haven: Yale University Press.
— (2013), 'France: World War Two', in A. Uhlmann (ed.), *Samuel Beckett in Context*, Cambridge: Cambridge University Press, pp. 109–25.
Gray, P. (1999), *Famine, Land and Politics: British Government and Irish Society, 1843–1850*, Dublin: Irish Academic Press.
Greven, D. (2018), 'Unlovely spectacle: D. A. Miller on *Call Me by Your Name*', *Film International*, 13 March, <https://filmint.nu/?p=23937> (last accessed 13 May 2020).

Gribben, D. (2008), 'Beckett's other revelation: "The Capital of the Ruins"', *Irish University Review*, 38.2, pp. 263–73.

Haddour, A. (2001), 'Introduction', in *Colonialism and Neocolonialism*, trans. S. Brewer, A. Haddour and T. McWilliams, New York: Routledge, pp. 1–16.

Halberstam, J. (2005), *In a Queer Time and Place: Transgender Bodies, Subcultural Lives*, New York: New York University Press.

— (2011), *The Queer Art of Failure*, Durham, NC: Duke University Press.

Happé, F. (1994), *Autism: An Introduction to Psychological Theory*, Cambridge, MA: Harvard University Press.

Hayles, K. (2005), *My Mother Is a Computer: Digital Subjects and Literary Texts*, Chicago: University of Chicago Press.

Heath, D. (2010), *Purifying Empire: Obscenity and the Politics of Moral Regulation in Britain, India and Australia*, Cambridge: Cambridge University Press.

Heffer, B. (2019), 'Beckett's queer atavism', in S. Kennedy (ed.), *Samuel Beckett and Biopolitics*, Special Issue of *Estudios Irlandeses*, 14.2, pp. 178–91.

Hobson, P. (2002), *The Cradle of Thought*, London: Macmillan.

Houston, L. (2019), 'Beckett in the dock: censorship, biopolitics and the Sinclair trial', in S. Kennedy (ed.), *Samuel Beckett and Biopolitics*, Special Issue of *Estudios Irlandeses*, 14.2, pp. 21–37.

Houston Jones, D. (2011), *Samuel Beckett and Testimony*, Basingstoke: Palgrave Macmillan.

Howes, M. (1996), *Yeats's Nations: Gender, Class, and Irishness*, Cambridge: Cambridge University Press.

Hug, C. (1999), *The Politics of Sexual Morality in Ireland*, New York: St. Martin's Press.

Huss, M. (1990), 'Pronatalism in the Inter-war Period in France', *Journal of Contemporary History* 25: 39–68.

Jeffers, J. (2009), *Beckett's Masculinity*, New York: Palgrave Macmillan.

Kanner, L. (1943), 'Autistic disturbances of affective contact', *Nervous Child*, 2, pp. 217–50.

Kant, I. [1788] (2015), *Critique of Practical Reason*, ed. and trans. M. Gregor, Cambridge: Cambridge University Press.

Kennedy, S. (2005), 'Cultural memory in *Mercier and Camier*: The fate of Noel Lemass', in M. Buning et al. (eds), *Historicising Beckett/Issues of Performance*, Special Issue of *Samuel Beckett Today/Aujourd'hui*, 15, pp. 117–31.

— (2010), '*First Love*: abortion and infanticide in Beckett and Yeats', in A. Moorjani et al. (eds), *Early Modern Beckett/Beckett et le début de l'ère moderne*, Special Issue of *Samuel Beckett Today/Aujourd'hui*, 22, pp. 79–91.

— (2014a), '"Bid us sigh on from day to day": Beckett and the Irish Big

House', in S. E. Gontarski (ed.), *The Edinburgh Companion to Beckett and the Arts*, Edinburgh: Edinburgh University Press, pp. 222–36.
— (2014b), '"Echo's Bones": Samuel Beckett after Yeats', in M. Howes and J. Valente (eds), *Yeats and Afterwords*, Indiana: Notre Dame University Press, pp. 276–305.
— (2019a), 'Mothering Molloy, or Beckett and cutlery', in D. Van Hulle and M. Nixon (eds), 'Beckett and the Everyday', *Journal of Beckett Studies*, 28.1, pp. 35–51.
— (ed.) (2019b), *Samuel Beckett and Biopolitics*, Special Issue of *Estudios Irlandeses*, 14.2.
Kennedy, S. and J. Valente (forthcoming), '"a form that accommodates the mess": degeneration and/as disability in Beckett's *Happy Days*', in M. Ellman, V. Mahaffey and S. White (eds), *The Edinburgh Companion to Irish Modernism*, Edinburgh, Edinburgh University Press.
Kennedy, S. and K. Weiss (eds) (2009), *Samuel Beckett: History, Memory, Archive*, New York: Palgrave Macmillan.
Kenner, H. (1973), *A Reader's Guide to Samuel Beckett*, New York: Farrar, Straus and Giroux.
Knowlson, J. (1996), *Damned to Fame: The Life of Samuel Beckett*, London: Bloomsbury.
Knowlson, J. and E. Knowlson (eds) (2007), *Beckett Remembering, Remembering Beckett*, London: Bloomsbury.
Kojève, A. (1969), *Introduction to the Reading of Hegel: Lectures on the Phenomenology of Spirit*, Ithaca: Cornell University Press.
Koonz, C. (2003), *The Nazi Conscience*, Cambridge, MA: Harvard University Press.
Kurasawa, F. (2014), 'In praise of ambiguity: on the visual economy of distant suffering', in R. Hadj-Moussa and M. Nijhawan (eds), *Suffering, Art, and Aesthetics*, Basingstoke: Palgrave Macmillan, pp. 23–50.
Le Sueur, D. (2001), 'Torture and decolonization of French Algeria: nationalism, "race" and violence during colonial incarceration', in G. Harper (ed.), *Colonial and Post-Colonial Incarceration*, London: Bloomsbury, pp. 161–75.
— (2005), *Uncivil War: Intellectuals and Identity Politics During the Decolonization of Algeria*, Lincoln, NE: University of Nebraska Press.
Lacan, J. (1988), *The Seminar of Jacques Lacan II: The Ego in Freud's Theory and in the Technique of Psychoanalysis, 1954–55*, trans. S. Tomaselli, New York: Norton.
— (1993), *The Seminar, Book III: The Psychoses, 1955–56*, trans. R. Grigg, London: Routledge.
— (1994), *Le Séminaire IV: La Relation d'Objet, 1956–57*, Paris, Éditions de Seuil.
Laplanche, J. (2011), 'Condensation and displacement', in *Freud and the Sexual*, New York: International Psychoanalytic Books, pp. 133–9.

Laplanche, J. and J. Pontalis (1973), *The Language of Psychoanalysis*, London: Hogarth Press.
Lazreg, M. (2008), *Torture and the Twilight of Empire: From Algiers to Baghdad*, Princeton: Princeton University Press.
Le Juez, B. (2009), *Beckett Before Beckett: Samuel Beckett's Lectures on French Literature*, London: Souvenir Press.
Lentin, R. (2016), 'Asylum seekers, Ireland, and the return of the repressed', *Irish Studies Review*, 24.1, pp. 21–34.
Levi, N. (2014), *Modernist Form and the Myth of Jewification*, New York: Fordham University Press.
Levin, Y. (2018), 'Univocity, exhaustion and failing better: reading Beckett with disability studies', *Journal of Beckett Studies*, 27.3, pp. 157–74.
Levy, E. (2011), 'The Beckettian mimesis of time', *University of Toronto Quarterly*, 80.1, pp. 89–107.
Linett, M. (2017), *Bodies of Modernism: Physical Disability in Transatlantic Modernist Literature*, Ann Arbor: University of Michigan Press.
Lloyd, D. (1995), *Anomalous States: Irish Writing and the Post-Colonial Moment*, Dublin: Lilliput Press.
— (2010), *Irish Culture and Colonial Modernity 1800–2000: The Transformation of Oral Space*, Cambridge: Cambridge University Press.
— (2019), *Under Representation: The Racial Regime of Aesthetics*, New York: Fordham University Press.
Loftis, S. (2017), *Imagining Autism*, Bloomington: Indiana University Press.
London, L. (2000), *Whitehall and the Jews, 1933–1948*, Cambridge: Cambridge University Press.
McCormack, W. J. (1994), *From Burke to Beckett: Ascendancy, Tradition and Betrayal*, Cork: Cork University Press.
McMillan, D. and M. Fehsenfeld (1988), *Beckett in the Theatre*, London: Calder.
McMullan, A. (2010), *Performing Embodiment in Samuel Beckett's Drama*, New York: Routledge.
McNaughton, J. (2009), 'Beckett's "brilliant obscurantics": *Watt* and the problem of propaganda', in S. Kennedy and K. Weiss (eds), *Samuel Beckett: History, Memory, Archive*, New York: Palgrave Macmillan, pp. 47–70.
— (2018), *Samuel Beckett and the Politics of Aftermath*, Oxford: Oxford University Press.
McRuer, R. (2006), *Crip Theory: Cultural Signs of Queerness and Disability*, New York: New York University Press.
Malthus, T. (1808), 'On the state of Ireland', *The Edinburgh Review*, 12, pp. 336–55.
Marrus, M. and R. Paxton (1981), *Vichy France and the Jews*, Stanford: Stanford University Press.
Maude, U. (2008), '"A stirring beyond coming and going": Beckett and Tourette's', *Journal of Beckett Studies*, 17.1–2, pp. 153–68.

— (2009), *Beckett, Technology and the Body*, Cambridge: Cambridge University Press.
Mayoux, J. (1979), 'Review of *How It Is*', in L. Graver and R. Federman (eds), *Samuel Beckett: The Critical Heritage*, London: Routledge and Kegan Paul, pp. 231–5.
Mehta, X. (1994), 'Ghosts', in L. Oppenheim (ed.), *Directing Beckett*, Ann Arbor: University of Michigan Press, pp. 170–85.
Melzack, R. (1975), 'The McGill Pain Questionnaire: major properties and scoring methods', *Pain*, 1.1, pp. 277–99.
Michaud, E. (2004), *The Cult of Art in Nazi Germany*, trans. J. Lloyd, Stanford: Stanford University Press.
Mikaberidze, A. (2013), *Atrocities, Massacres, and War Crimes: An Encyclopaedia, Vol. I*, Oxford: ABC-CLIO.
Milhous, J. and R. Hume (1985), *Producible Interpretation: Eight English Plays, 1675–1707*, Carbondale: Southern Illinois University Press.
Miller, T. (2000), 'Beckett's political technology: expression, confession and torture in the later drama', *Samuel Beckett Today/Aujourd'hui*, 9, pp. 255–78.
Mitchell, A. (2010), *Heidegger Among the Sculptors: Body, Space, and the Art of Dwelling*, Stanford: Stanford University Press.
Mitchell, D. T. with S. L. Snyder (2015), *The Biopolitics of Disability: Neoliberalism, Ablenationalism and Peripheral Embodiment*, Ann Arbor: University of Michigan Press.
Mollow, A. (2012), 'Is sex disability? Queer theory and the disability drive', in R. McRuer and A. Mollow (eds), *Sex and Disability*, Durham, NC: Duke University Press, pp. 285–312.
Morash, C. and S. Richards (2013), *Mapping Irish Theatre: Theories of Space and Place*, Cambridge: Cambridge University Press.
Morin, E. (2009), *Samuel Beckett and the Problem of Irishness*, New York: Palgrave Macmillan.
— (2014), 'Odds, ends, beginnings: Samuel Beckett and theatre cultures in 1930s Dublin', in S. E. Gontarski (ed.), *The Edinburgh Companion to Samuel Beckett and the Arts*, Edinburgh: Edinburgh University Press, pp. 209–21.
— (2015), '*Endgame* and shorter plays: religious, political and other readings', in D. Van Hulle (ed.), *The New Cambridge Companion to Samuel Beckett*, Cambridge: Cambridge University Press, pp. 60–72.
— (2017), *Beckett's Political Imagination*, Cambridge: Cambridge University Press.
Moscoso, J. (2012), *Pain: A Cultural History*, Basingstoke: Palgrave Macmillan.
Müller, K. (2014), '"Violet vomiting over me": Ernst Barlach and National Socialist cultural policy', in O. Peters (ed.), *Degenerate Art: The Attack on Modern Art in Nazi Germany*, Munich: Prestel, pp. 176–85.

Muñoz, J. (2009), *Cruising Utopia: The Then and There of Queer Futurity*, New York: New York University Press.

Nadeau, M. (1979), 'Review of *How It Is*', in L. Graver and R. Federman (eds), *Samuel Beckett: The Critical Heritage*, London: Routledge and Kegan Paul, pp. 224–8.

Nashat, G. and J. Tucker (1998), *Women in the Middle East and North Africa: Restoring Women to History*, Indianapolis: Indiana University Press.

Nietzsche, F. [1887] (1966), *Beyond Good and Evil*, trans. W. Kaufman, New York: Random House.

— [1886] (2003), *The Genealogy of Morals*, London: Dover Press.

Nixon, M. (2011), *Samuel Beckett's German Diaries 1936–37*, London: Continuum.

Nordau, M. [1892] (1993), *Degeneration*, London: Heinemann.

Noys, B. (2015), 'Vital texts and bare life: the uses and abuses of life in contemporary fiction', *CounterText*, 1.2, pp. 169–85.

Ó Gráda, C. (1999), *Black '47 and Beyond: The Great Irish Famine in History, Economy, and Memory*, Princeton: Princeton University Press.

Park, C. (1967), *The Siege*, Boston: Little, Brown.

Pavard, B. (2019), 'The right to know? The politics of information about contraception in France (1950s–80s)', *Medical History*, 63.2, pp. 173–88.

Pearson, N. (2001), '"Outside of here it's death": co-dependency and the ghosts of decolonization in Beckett's *Endgame*', *ELH*, 68.1, pp. 215–39.

Perelman, B. (1993), 'Parataxis and narrative: the new sentence in theory and practice', *American Literature*, 65.2, pp. 313–24.

Perloff, M. (1996), *Wittgenstein's Ladder*, Chicago: University of Chicago Press.

— (2005), 'In love with hiding: Samuel Beckett's war', *The Iowa Review*, 35.1, pp. 76–103.

Phillips, A. (1995), 'Symptoms', in *Terrors and Experts*, Cambridge, MA: Harvard University Press, pp. 33–46.

Phillips, J. (1999), *Forbidden Fictions: Pornography and Censorship in Twentieth-Century French Literature*, London: Pluto Press.

Piette, A. (2016), 'Torture, text, human rights: Beckett's *Comment c'est/How It Is* and the Algerian War', in A. Hepburn (ed.), *Around 1945: Literature, Citizenship, Human Rights*, London: McGill-Queen's University Press, pp. 151–74.

Pilling, J. (1994), 'Beckett's English fiction', in J. Pilling (ed.), *The Cambridge Companion to Beckett*, Cambridge: Cambridge University Press, pp. 17–42.

— (1998), 'Guesses and recesses: notes on, in and towards *Dream of Fair to Middling Women*', *Samuel Beckett Today/Aujourd'hui*, 7.1, pp. 13–24.

— (1999), *Beckett's* Dream *Notebook*, Reading: Reading University Press.

Pountney, R. (1988), *Theatre of Shadows: Samuel Beckett's Drama, 1956–1976*, Gerards Cross: Colin Smythe.

Presner, T. (2003), '"Clear heads, solid stomachs, and hard muscles": Max Nordau and the aesthetics of Jewish regeneration', *Modernism/Modernity*, 10.2, pp. 269–96.
Pryor, J. (2017), *Time Slips: Queer Temporalities, Contemporary Performance, and the Hole of History*, Evanston, IL: Northwestern University Press.
Purcell, S. (2015), '"Buckled discourses": disability and degeneration in Beckett's *More Pricks Than Kicks*', *Samuel Beckett Today/Aujourd'hui*, 27.1, pp. 29–41.
— (2019), 'Beckett and disability biopolitics: the case of Cuchulain', in S. Kennedy (ed.), *Samuel Beckett and Biopolitics*, Special Issue of *Estudios Irlandeses*, 14.2, pp. 52–64.
Quayson, A. (2007), *Aesthetic Nervousness*, New York: Columbia University Press.
— (2010), 'Autism, narrative and emotion: on Samuel Beckett's *Murphy*', *University of Toronto Quarterly*, 79.2, pp. 838–62.
Quinan, C. (2014), 'Uses and abuses of gender and nationality: torture and the French-Algerian War', in S. Ponzanesi (ed.), *Gender, Globalization, and Violence: Postcolonial Conflict Zones*, London: Routledge, pp. 111–25.
Ramachandran, V. (2011), *The Tell-Tale Brain*, New York: Norton.
Reason, M. and D. Reynolds (2010), 'Kinesthesia, empathy and related pleasures: an inquiry into audience experiences of watching dance', *Dance Research Journal*, 42.2, pp. 49–75.
Reggiani, A. H. (2007), *God's Eugenicist: Alexis Carrel and the Sociobiology of Decline*, New York: Berghahn Books.
Rejali, D. (2007), 'Torture makes the man', *South Central Review*, 24.1, pp. 151–69.
— (2009), *Torture and Democracy*, Princeton: Princeton University Press.
Reyes, X. (2016), *Horror Film and Affect: Towards a Corporeal Model of Viewership*, London: Routledge.
Ricoeur, P. (1984–8), *Time and Narrative*, vols 1–3, trans. K. Blamey and D. Pellauer, Chicago: University of Chicago Press.
Ross, K. (1995), *Fast Cars, Clean Bodies: Decolonization and the Reordering of French Culture*, Cambridge, MA: MIT Press.
Rousso, H. (1991), *The Vichy Syndrome: History and Memory in France since 1944*, trans. A. Goldhammer, Cambridge, MA: Harvard University Press.
Rozga, A., S. Anderson and D. Robins (2011), 'Major current neuropsychological theories of autism', in D. Fein (ed.), *The Neuropsychology of Autism*, Oxford: Oxford University Press, pp. 104–7.
Salisbury, L. (2008), '"What is the word": Beckett's aphasic modernism', *Journal of Beckett Studies*, 17.1–2, pp. 78–126.
— (2014), 'Gloria SMH and Beckett's linguistic encryptions', in S. E. Gontarski (ed.), *The Edinburgh Companion to Samuel Beckett and the Arts*, Edinburgh: Edinburgh University Press, pp. 153–68.

Salisbury, L. and C. Code (2016), 'Jackson's parrot: Samuel Beckett, aphasic speech, automatisms, and psychosomatic language', in E. Barry, U. Maude and L. Salisbury (eds), *Beckett, Medicine and the Brain*, Special Issue of *Journal of Medical Humanities*, 37.2, pp. 205–22.

Sartre, J.-P. (2001a), 'Colonialism is a system', in *Colonialism and Neocolonialism*, trans. S. Brewer, A. Haddour and T. McWilliams, New York: Routledge, pp. 30–47.

— (2001b), 'A victory', in *Colonialism and Neocolonialism*, trans. S. Brewer, A. Haddour and T. McWilliams, New York: Routledge, pp. 65–77.

Scarry, E. (1985), *The Body in Pain: The Making and Unmaking of the World*, Oxford: Oxford University Press.

Schopenhauer, A. [1850] (2004), *On the Suffering of the World*, trans. R. J. Hollingdale, London: Penguin.

Schreibman, L. (2005), *The Science and Fiction of Autism*, Cambridge, MA: Harvard University Press.

Shakespeare, W. [1611] (1988), *The Tempest*, ed. F. Kermode, London: Arden.

Sheehan, P. (2002), *Modernism, Narrative and Humanism*, Cambridge: Cambridge University Press.

— (2009), 'A world without monsters: Beckett and the ethics of cruelty', in R. Smith (ed.), *Beckett and Ethics*, London: Bloomsbury, pp. 86–101.

Shenker, I. (1979), 'An interview with Beckett', in L. Graver and R. Federman (eds), *Samuel Beckett: The Critical Heritage*, London: Routledge and Kegan Paul, pp. 146–9.

Shepard, T. (2006), *The Invention of Decolonization: The Algerian War and the Remaking of France*, London: Cornell University Press.

Siebers, T. (2010), *Disability Aesthetics*, Ann Arbor, University of Michigan Press.

Sigel, L. Z. (2002), *Governing Pleasures: Pornography and Social Change in England, 1815–1914*, New Brunswick: Rutledge University Press.

— (2011), 'Censorship in Inter-War Britain: Obscenity, Spectacle, and the Workings of the Liberal State,' *Journal of Social History* 45.1: 61–83.

— (2013), 'Censorship and Magic Tricks in Inter-War Britain,' *La Revue LISA/LISA E-Journal* 11.1: 72–92.

Skultans, V. (2007), *Empathy and Healing: Essays in Medical and Narrative Anthropology*, Oxford and New York: Berghahn Books.

Slade, J. W. (2001), *Pornography and Sexual Representation: A Reference Guide, Volume II*, Westport: Greenwood Press.

Smith, J. (2004), 'The politics of sexual knowledge: the origin of Ireland's containment culture and the Carrigan Report (1931)', *Journal of the History of Sexuality*, 13.2, pp. 208–33.

Snyder, S. and D. Mitchell (2006), *Cultural Locations of Disability*, Chicago: University of Chicago Press.

— (2010), 'Introduction: ablenationalism and the geo-politics of disability', *Journal of Literary and Cultural Disability Studies*, 4.2, pp. 113–25.

Spenser, E. [1596] (1918), 'A View of the Present State of Ireland', in *The Works of Edmund Spenser*, ed. R. Morris, London: Macmillan, pp. 609–83.
Stanfield, P. (1988), *Yeats and Politics in the 1930s*, Basingstoke: Macmillan.
Stewart, P. (2011), *Sex and Aesthetics in Samuel Beckett's Work*, New York: Palgrave Macmillan.
— (2016), 'The politics of form in Samuel Beckett's late theatre and prose', *European Journal of English Studies*, 20:3, pp. 263–74.
Strickland, G. (1979), 'Roland Barthes's poem of love', *Cambridge Quarterly*, 9.1, pp. 70–6.
Sugimoto, B. (2017), 'Beckett, *Bildung*, and the modernist *Bildungsroman*', in N. Bowe, M. Bariselli and W. Davies (eds), *Samuel Beckett and Europe*, Newcastle: Cambridge Scholars, pp. 77–98.
Surkis, J. (2010), 'Ethics and violence: Simone de Beauvoir, Djamila Boupacha, and the Algerian War', *French Politics, Culture, and Society*, 28.2, pp. 38–55.
Tagg, J. (1993), *The Burden of Representation: Essays on Photographies and Histories*, Minneapolis: University of Minnesota Press.
Taylor, D. (2007), 'Double-blind: the torture case', *Critical Inquiry*, 33.4, pp. 710–33.
Teekell, A. (2016), 'Beckett in purgatory: "unspeakable" *Watt* and the Second World War', *Twentieth-Century Literature*, 62.3, pp. 247–70.
Thiébault, M. (1957), 'Deux grenades explosent dans la casbah. Un mort et vingt et un blessés' [Two grenades explode in the Casbah. One dead and five injured], 5 November, *Le Monde Archives*, <https://www.lemonde.fr/archives/article/1957/11/05/deux-grenades-explosent-dans-la-casbah-un-mort-et-vingt-et-un-blesses_3133914_1819218.html> (last accessed 13 May 2020).
Tremain, S. (2017), *Foucault and Feminist Philosophy of Disability*, Ann Arbor: University of Michigan Press.
Trevelyan, C. (1848), 'The Irish crisis', *The Edinburgh Review*, 175, pp. 1–201.
Valente, J. (2002), *Dracula's Crypt: Bram Stoker, Irishness, and the Question of Blood*, Urbana: University of Illinois Press.
— (2011), *The Myth of Manliness in Irish National Culture, 1880–1922*, Urbana: University of Illinois Press.
— (2013), 'Modernism and cognitive disability: a genealogy', in J. Rabaté (ed.), *A Handbook of Modernism Studies*, Chichester: Wiley-Blackwell, pp. 379–98.
Vince, N. (2015), *Our Fighting Sisters: Nation, Memory and Gender in Algeria, 1954–2012*, Manchester: Manchester University Press.
Warner, M. (1993), 'Introduction', in M. Warner (ed.), *Fear of a Queer Planet: Queer Politics and Social Theory*, Minneapolis: University of Minnesota Press, pp. vii–xxxi.
Wheatley, D. (2013), '"Quite exceptionally anthropoid": species anxiety

and metamorphosis in Beckett's humans and other animals', in M. Brydon (ed.), *Beckett and Animals*, Cambridge: Cambridge University Press, pp. 59–70.

Whelan, I. (1995), 'The stigma of souperism', in C. Póirtéir (ed.), *The Great Irish Famine: The Thomas Davis Lecture Series*, Dublin: Mercier Press, pp. 135–54.

White, H. (1978), *Tropics of Discourse: Essays in Cultural Criticism*, Baltimore: Johns Hopkins University Press.

— (1980), 'The value of narrativity in the representation of reality', *Critical Inquiry*, 7.1, pp. 5–27.

— (1987), *The Content of the Form: Narrative Discourse and Historical Representation*, Baltimore: Johns Hopkins University Press.

Whitelaw, B. (1995), *Billie Whitelaw... Who He?* New York: St. Martin's Press.

Williams, R. (2006) *Modern Tragedy*, ed. P. McCallum, Broadview Encore Editions, 2006.

Wilson, J. (2008), *Weather Reports from the Autism Front*, Jefferson: McFarland.

Yeats, W. B. (1961), *Essays and Introductions*, New York: Macmillan.

— [1937] (1962), *A Vision*, London: Macmillan.

Zuschlag, C. (1997), 'Censorship in the visual arts in Nazi Germany', in E. C. Childs (ed.), *Suspended Licence: Censorship and the Visual Arts*, Seattle: University of Washington Press, pp. 210–43.

Notes on Contributors

Nic Barilar is a PhD candidate in theatre and performance studies at the University of Pittsburgh. His dissertation rethinks censorship as mobile by tracing transnational performance histories of banned Irish plays. Recent theatre projects include Beckett's *Footfalls* and *Catastrophe* for the University of Pittsburgh (director), *Ragtime* at Lincoln Park Performing Arts Center (as 'Father'), and the North American premiere of Máiréad Ní Ghráda's *On Trial* (producer and director).

James Brophy teaches at the University of Maine where he is Lecturer in the department of Modern Languages and Classics and Preceptor in the Honors College. His work has appeared in *Twentieth-Century Literature*, *Journal of Translation Studies* and *Paideuma: Modern and Contemporary Poetry and Poetics*, among other venues. He is currently co-editing a book on the poetry of Samuel Beckett with W. Davies.

William Davies is a literary critic and historian. His books on Samuel Beckett include *Samuel Beckett and the Second World War* (2020), *Beckett and Politics* (2020, edited with Helen Bailey) and *The Poetry of Samuel Beckett* (forthcoming, edited with J. Brophy). He is an English editor of *LONGITŪDINĒS* magazine. He works at the University of Reading

Byron Heffer received his PhD from the University of Sussex in 2019. His dissertation research, funded by the Consortium of the Humanities and the Arts South-east England (CHASE), studied atavism, posthumanism and the politics of declining life in the work of Wyndham Lewis, Mina Loy and Samuel Beckett. His essay 'Beckett's Queer Atavism' appeared in a special issue of *Estudios Irlandeses* on *Samuel Beckett and Biopolitics*.

Seán Kennedy is Professor of English and Coordinator of Irish Studies at Saint Mary's University, Halifax, Nova Scotia. His recent publications include, as editor, *Samuel Beckett and Biopolitics* (2019) and, as co-editor with P. Bixby, *(Dis)embodied Beckett* (2018).

Hannah Simpson teaches and researches in the faculty of English at the University of Oxford. Her scholarship focuses on modern and contemporary theatre and performance, particularly the representation of pain and disability, and the work of Samuel Beckett. She is preparing a monograph entitled *Witnessing Pain: Samuel Beckett and Post-War Francophone Theatre*.

Joseph Valente is UB Distinguished Professor at SUNY-Buffalo and Treasurer of the International Yeats Society. He is the author of *James Joyce and the Problem of Justice: Negotiating Sexual and Colonial Difference*, *Dracula's Crypt: Bram Stoker, Irishness, and the Question of Blood* and *The Myth of Manliness in Irish National Culture, 1880–1922*. Most recently, he has co-authored, with M. Backus, *The Child Sex Scandal and Modern Irish Literature: Writing the Unspeakable*, forthcoming from Indiana University Press (2020). He is editor of several volumes, including *Quare Joyce*, *Urban Ireland*, *Ireland in Psychoanalysis* (with S. Kennedy and M. Todd) and *Yeats and Afterwords* (with M. Howes).

Dominic Walker is a Leverhulme Early Career Fellow at the University of Cambridge. His project is 'Underwriting the Market: A Literary Genealogy of Modern Economic Thought'. His PhD, 'Samuel Beckett and Economics', was undertaken at the University of Sussex. His recent publications include 'Black Markets: Beckett's Bad Equilibrium' (2018) and 'The Theme of the Five Biscuits: *Murphy*, Foucault, and Beckett's Critique of Neoliberalism' (2019).

Index

ablenationalism, 8, 10–11
Ackerley, C. J., 22, 27, 33, 36, 100
Adorno, Theodor, 36, 128
Africa, 66, 128
Agamben, Giorgio, 50, 54–6
Algeria, 4, 117–32
America, 66
Anderton, Joseph, 55
Arnaud, Georges, 121
Attridge, Derek, 65
Austen, Jane, 36, 37
Australia, 66
autism, 14, 16–32

Bacon, Francis, 54–8
Badiou, Alain, 102
Balzac, Honoré de, 36–40, 42, 45
Barilar, Nic, 3, 105–16
Barlach, Ernst, 52, 53
Baron-Cohen, Simon, 18, 20
Barry, Elizabeth, 12, 80
Barthes, Roland, 3, 35, 44, 54, 90–104
Beckett, Frank, 5
Beckett, Samuel
   Dream of Fair to Middling Women, 1, 7, 33–46
   Endgame, 3, 11, 62–78, 90–104, 128
   Happy Days, 3, 12, 105–116
   How it is, 117–132
   La peinture de van Velde ou le monde et le pantalon, 77
   Malone Dies, 2, 33, 66
   More Pricks Than Kicks, 6
   Murphy, 2, 14, 16–32
   Premier Amour/First Love, 8
   The Unnamable, 10, 11, 33 47–61, 78, 113
   Three Novels, 56, 57, 117
   Waiting for Godot, 3, 33, 79–89, 109, 117, 129
   Watt, 10, 33–46, 62–4, 72–6
Belkacem, Krim, 129
Bersani, Leo, 2, 13, 111
Bhabha, Homi, 66
Bildungsroman, 39, 41–3
biopolitics, 10-11, 47–61, 62–79
Bixby, Patrick, 12, 34, 43
Blin, Roger, 86
Bouhired, Djamila, 121–3
Boupacha, Djamila, 117, 122–5
Bourdieu, Pierre, 77
Boxall, Peter, 3, 93
Branche, Raphaëlle, 118, 122, 128
Bray, Barbara, 122
Brooke, Stephen, 114, 127
Brophy, James, 3, 90–104
Burroughs, William, 54–5, 60

Carleton, William, 73–7
Carlyle, Thomas, 66
Carrigan, James, 9
Carville, Conor, 39, 41
Catanzaro, Mary, 91, 93
Catholic, 68, 70–2, 119

Cavell, Stanley, 91, 93–4
censorship, 8, 9, 49, 51–2, 114
Chiang, Michelle, 107
chrononormativity, 109–11
Cixous, Hélène, 121
Clanricarde, Lord, 75
Clarendon, Lord, 75
Code, Christopher, 5, 6
Cohn, Ruby, 129
colonial, 8–9, 11, 62–78, 118–20
colonialism, *see* colonial
Connor, Steven, 86
Cork, 72
Corkery, Daniel, 1, 8–10
Critchley, Simon, 2, 88
Curtis, L. P., 71
Cyprus, 128

Dada, 52
Daly, Mary, 114
Davidson, Arnold, 7
Davidson, Michael, 12–13
Davies, William, 10, 33–6, 80
de Beauvoir, Simone, 117, 122–5
Dean, Tim, 7–8, 14
degenerate, 1, 6, 10–11, 47–61
Deutsch, Helene, 58
Dickens, Charles, 36
disability, 6–8, 12–15, 16–32, 47–62, 93
Dolan, Jill, 109
Donnelly, James, 75
Dowd, Garin, 84
Driver, Tom, 15
Durantaye, Leland de la, 37
Duthuit, Georges, 79

Edelman, Lee, 13
Effinger, Elizabeth, 55
Eggers-Kestner, Kurt, 40
erotic, 8, 27, 93–4
Esposito, Roberto, 50, 61
eugenics, 47–9, 51
Evangelicalism, 62–79
Expressionism, 68

famine, 11, 62–78
Fascist, 10, 11, 35, 47–61, 77, 118
Felman, Shoshana, 35, 42, 43
Ferriter, Diarmuid, 114
Filgate, Fitzherbert, 72
Fillingim, Robert B., 81
Forti, Simona, 10, 50
Foucault, Michel, 9, 14, 48, 54–5, 60, 63, 67, 108
France, 3, 10, 38, 44, 73, 80, 84, 114, 117, 120, 123,
Freeman, Elizabeth, 108
Freemans Journal, The, 75
Freud, Sigmund, 2–8, 13–14, 52
Frith, U., 18

Gallese, Vittorio, 87
Garner, Stanton B., 107, 110
Garrison, Alysia, 56–7
Germany, 10, 34–7, 40, 51–2, 59, 77
Gibson, Andrew, 10, 38, 44, 47, 55, 62, 80, 102, 117
Gierow, Karl Ragnar, 33–4, 81
Gilbert, P. and J. Mascaro, 84
Goebbels, Joseph, 51
Goldman, A., 87
Gontarski, S. E., 33, 36, 37, 100, 112,
Gooch, George Peabody, 37
Gordon, Lois, 71, 81
Gray, Peter, 62–78
Grey, Earl, 69
Great Britain, 66, 114
Gregory, William, 75
Gribben, Darren, 12, 140

Halberstam, Jack, 3, 108–11
Halimi, Gisèle, 117, 124–5
Hall, Peter, 81
Happé, Francesca, 18
Hardy, Thomas, 21
Hayles, K., 21
Heath, Deana, 112, 114
Heffer, Byron, 3, 10–12, 47–61
Hegel, G.F., 39, 40, 121
heterosexual, 3, 7, 108, 90, 93–4

Hitler, Adolf, 10, 11, 47–51, 59, 63–4, 77
  Mein Kampf, 59
Hobson, P., 18, 140
Holocaust, The 66
homoerotic, 3, 93
homosexual, 3, 10, 49, 90, 93–4, 118, 121, 122, 123
homosexuality, *see* homosexual
Houston, Lloyd (Maedhbh), 9
Howard, Richard, 134
Howes, Marjorie, 37, 65
Hug, C., 114
human, 47–61, 66, 74, 75, 79–81, 87–9, 93, 111, 119–123, 127–8
humanism, 13, 39

Ibsen, Henrik, 78
India, 64, 140
Ireland, 8–10, 34, 37, 44, 62–78, 80, 114
Ireland, Northern, 80, 128

James, William, 27
Jeffers, Jennifer, 105, 110
Joyce, James, 5, 6, 39

Kafka, Franz, 59
Kanner, Leo, 17
Kant, Immanuel, 25, 126
Kempis, Thomas à, 2, 6
Kennedy, Seán, 1–15, 33, 34, 40, 62–78, 80, 113
Kenner, Hugh, 92, 97
Kerry, 72
Kingsley, Charles, 66
Kipling, Rudyard, 78
Knowlson, James, 8, 11, 37, 73, 86, 105, 129, 130
Kojève, Alexandre, 29
Koonz, Claudia, 36, 37
Kurasawa, F., 84

Lacan, Jacques, 13–14, 27
Lamarck, Jean-Baptiste, 2

Laplanche, Jean, 65, 77
Lartéguy, Jean, 122
Lazreg, M., 122
Le Sueur, D., 119, 122
Lehár, Franz, 116
Lentin, Ronit, 9
Les Temps Modernes, 119
Levin, Yael, 12
Levy, Eric P., 107
Lindon, Jérôme, 119, 121
Linett, Maren, 53–4
Lloyd, David, 4, 8–9, 66, 117–132
Loftis, S., 17
London, 1, 26, 71, 105

McCormack, W. J., 8, 72
McGreevy, Thomas, 1–2, 4–6, 25, 39
McMillan, Douglas and Martha Fehsenfeld, 91–2, 98
McNaughton, James, 2, 10–11, 33–46, 62–78, 109, 113
McSwiney, Terence, 66
Malthus, Thomas, 74
Manet, Édouard, 54, 55, 59
Marrus, M. and R. Paxton, 84
Massu, Jacques, 123
Maude, Ulrika, 12, 86
Mauriac, Francois, 119
Mayo, 72, 75
Mayoux, Jean-Jacques, 123
Mehta, Xerxes, 85, 86
Melzack, R., 82
metrocolonial, 62–78
Michaud, Eric, 10, 51, 58–9
Mikaberidze, A., 121
Miller, Tyrus, 4
Mitchell, Andrew, 52–3
Mitchell, David and Sharon Snyder, 8
Mitchell, John, 68
Mitchell, Pamela, 118, 129–30
Moll, Albert, 7
Mollow, Anna, 8, 13–14
Moore, George Henry, 83
Morash, Chris and Shaun Richards, 107, 110

Morin, Emilie, 4, 33, 37, 62, 64, 91–2, 113
Muñoz, José, 109

Nadeau, Maurice, 161, 123–4
narrative, 10–11, 16, 24, 25, 31, 33–46, 48, 57, 64–5, 69, 71, 78, 97, 99
Nashat, J. and G. Tucker, 121, 122
Nazi, 10, 11, 33–46, 47–61, 63–4, 73, 80, 84, 119–20
Nazism, *see* Nazi
Nietzsche, Friedrich, 11, 67
Nixon, Mark, 10, 35, 40, 51, 58–9
Nordau, Max, 2, 5–6, 47, 49–50
normal, 1–15, 57, 60, 79, 90, 109–116, 117–132
normalising, *see* normal
normative, 14, 23, 29, 31, 36, 48, 54, 55, 60, 108, 114, 119, 131
Noys, Benjamin, 54–5, 60

Ó Gráda, Cormac, 68–9
Oram, Harold, 129

Park, Clara Claiborne, 31
Pavard, B., 114
Pearson, Nels, 63
Perelman, Bob, 41
Péron, Alfred, 78
Phillips, Adam, 2
Phillips, J., 114
Piette, Adam, 118–20, 128
Pilling, John, 2, 34, 37, 47
Pim, Jonathan, 71
Plato, 10, 54, 59–60, 95
Pontalis, J.B., 77
Pountney, Rosemary, 117
Protestant, 68–72, 77
Protestant Colonisation Society, 72
Pryor, Jaclyn, 108–9
psychoanalysis, 1–15, 31, 65
psychosocial, 17, 27, 28
Purcell, Siobhán, 6, 8, 12, 47–8, 53, 59

Quayson, Ato, 14, 16–32
queer, 3, 8, 9, 91–104, 105–116
queerness, *see* queer
Quinan, Christine, 121, 125

Ramachandran, V., 18
Reggiani, A. H., 84
republicanism, 11, 16
Reyes, X., 79, 87
Ricoeur, Paul, 35
Roe, Samuel Robinson, 73
Rosenberg, Alfred, 52
Ross, K., 114, 123–4
Rousseau, Jean-Jacques, 25
Rousso, H., 80
Rozga, A., 18
Russell, Bertrand, 121
Russell, Lord, 68, 75

sadism, 119, 129
Saint-Lô, 12, 15
Salan, Raoul, 128
Salisbury, Laura, 5, 6, 12
Sartre, Jean-Paul, 119–21, 131
Scarry, Elaine, 3, 82–3
Schopenhauer, Arthur, 3, 79–80, 87
Schreibman, Susan, 17
Shakespeare, William, 76
Sheehan, Paul, 45, 47, 51, 106
Shenker, Israel, 58, 59
Shepard, T., 117, 119
Siebers, Tobin, 14, 48–9, 51–2
Sigel, L.Z., 114
Simpson, Hannah, 2, 4, 79–89
Smith, Adam, 69
Smith, Barbara Hernstein, 35
Smith, James, 9
Snyder, Sharon and David Mitchell, 9, 12–14, 48
Soustelle, Jacques, 119
Spenser, Edmund, 68
Stalin, Josef, 10–11, 63–4, 68, 77
Stanfield, Paul, 37
Stieve, Friedrich, 35–7, 42
Strickland, George, 93–4

Sugimoto, Bunshiro, 39
Surkis, Judith, 120–21, 124–5
symptoms, 1–8, 17, 47

Tagg, C., 114
Teekell, Anna, 34
torture, 4, 12, 56, 117–132
Tremain, Shelley, 13–14
Trevelyan, Charles, 69, 73
Trinity College, Dublin, 34, 37, 39

Valente, Joseph, 2, 6, 13–14, 16–32, 70–1, 74
Vergès, Jacques, 121
Vichy, 10, 38, 44, 105, 117
Victorian, 65, 74, 92, 105
Vince, N., 121, 122

violence, 36, 50, 56, 59, 61, 68, 80, 94, 109, 111–13, 116, 117–32

Walker, Dominic, 4, 117–32
Warner, Michael, 109
Weber, Max, 2
Westminster, 71
Whelan, Irene, 72, 77
White, Hayden, 35, 44
Whitelaw, Billie, 105–6
Williams, Raymond, 80
Wilson, J., 19
Wood, Charles, 90, 100

Yeats, William Butler, 11, 34, 37–8, 40

Zuschlag, Christoph, 51

EU representative:
Easy Access System Europe
Mustamäe tee 50, 10621 Tallinn, Estonia
Gpsr.requests@easproject.com

www.ingramcontent.com/pod-product-compliance
Lightning Source LLC
Chambersburg PA
CBHW070359240426
43671CB00013BA/2565